June 24, 2014

Dearest Jean,

ELLEVIE

Wishing you good travel through the lines of my life.

Love
Marcell...

ELLEVIE

A
TRUE STORY
of Repressed Memories
and Multiple Personality Disorder

MARCELLE EVIE GUY
CO-WRITTEN BY G.S. PAYNE

Blue Fluke Media

Ellevie
A True Story of Repressed Memories and Multiple Personality Disorder
Marcelle Evie Guy & G.S. Payne

Hardcover ISBN: 978-1-939288-60-8
eBook ISBN: 978-1-939288-61-5
Library of Congress Control Number: 2014938143

www.MarcelleGuy.com

Family Photo on Jacket: Photo Scan and Restore by Mike Delaney, Sonoma, CA

Published by Blue Fluke Media,
An Imprint of Wyatt-MacKenzie

Blue Fluke Media

DEDICATION

For my children,
for they could not understand.

This is a true story. I have endeavored to recreate, as accurately as possible, events, locales, and conversations from my memories of them. However, in order to protect their privacy, I have changed the names of individuals in certain instances. M.G.

TABLE OF CONTENTS

P R O L O G U E

~

THE NUN, IN HER BLACK ROBE AND HABIT, APPEARED like an ink spot in a room of white beds and white linens. The body of the little girl on the bed the nun was seated beside was frail and lifeless. Her arms were stretched out above her head, her hands tied to the headboard. Five votive prayer candles had been placed on her bare chest. A strange circumstance—the candles, in their small glass jars, had been placed upside down. An element, perhaps, of a bizarre exorcism practice. Or more likely some obscure ritual for the dead. For surely the girl could not have been living. One thing that would have made that impossible was the fact that she was being spied on from above, from the ceiling, by herself, in an out-of-body way. And the little girl's Catholic teaching made it very clear that the separation of the soul occurs only at death.

~

IN 1977, AT THE AGE OF FORTY-TWO, I was standing in the kitchen of my home in Petaluma, California. For close to two years I'd been trying to come to grips with the strange things that had been happening to me. A psychosomatic paralysis had taken me on a journey first to my family doctor, then to a psychiatrist. Under hypnosis I'd apparently relived some forgotten incident. I'd thrashed wildly about, arms punching the air, fighting something or someone, though I knew not what or whom. In time I would have my suspicions, though for a while I would manage— somehow—to keep the suspicions both to myself and from myself. Then came a bewildering and stunning flashback, a recollection of a newspaper headline. A certain murder from years ago. The sudden revelations were vague and confusing and overwhelming. Something was happening to me, and I didn't know what it was.

That day, standing by the counter in my kitchen, the image of the little dead girl came to me again, as it had hundreds, perhaps thousands of times before. I had carried it with me most of my life. It was a part of me, a part I never questioned. It was just there. But certain recent experiences, including the flashback, had somehow awakened something within and suddenly, unexpectedly, I was overcome with the distinct awareness that the little girl in the image was not, in fact, dead. She was quite alive, and I knew this definitively because, all at once, I recognized her. The little girl was me at the age of seven, forgotten, abandoned, for thirty-five years.

"She did not die," I cried aloud. "She is alive. The little girl on the bed. She is alive. Oh my God, *I* am alive!"

In the days to come my revelation, a not unhappy one, would nevertheless become unnerving, and then downright frightening. The sudden inclusion into my life of the little girl, and all that she would come to represent, was much more than I could handle. My instincts told me to run, but wasn't that what I had done my whole life? The little girl had found me. There was no longer a place to run from her, no longer a place to hide. I was losing control. The following days were full of anxiety and dread; at night sleep became impossible for fear that I would awaken not as me, but as somebody else.

There would be visits to psychiatrists and one particularly unproductive stay in a psychiatric ward. But things became worse.

One morning I drove desperately towards my counselor Jim Fraser's Santa Rosa office, my ability to maintain control of my life collapsing from within. My car wandered between lanes and I had to force myself to concentrate, to focus on where I was going and to watch for the exit I needed. On the radio, Petula Clark was singing. *The lights are much brighter there…you can forget all your troubles, forget all your cares and go downtown…things'll be great when you're downtown.* It was delightfully incongruous and suddenly I was in the passing lane, ready to skirt past the exit and head for where the lights are brighter, to where I could forget all my troubles. I wanted to be downtown. I wanted to run some more. I caught myself in time and swerved back into the exit lane.

At Jim's office I explained breathlessly that I could not go home. I needed a secure environment. I needed safety. I needed to be admitted to the psychiatric hospital again. He asked why. "Because there is a little girl in me," I explained, "and she wants to take over."

CHAPTER ONE

Lac-Mégantic

∾

LAC-MÉGANTIC IS A SMALL TOWN NAMED AFTER THE
lake on which it sits. The lake ("lac" in French, of course, for
it is situated in the province of Quebec where French is the
primary language) is a pristine, 10.2 square mile body of
fresh and clear water, 160 miles east of Montréal and 120
miles south of Quebec City. It is roughly only ten miles from
the state of Maine, to the east. In that direction lies the small
township of Frontenac, where my family had a summer
home. South of the lake is the village of Woburn where my
maternal grandparents raised their family, my grandmother
having been born in Haydenville, Massachusetts, and her
grandparents having emigrated from France.

There is a fair amount of civic pride shared by the
population of roughly six thousand in Lac-Mégantic, and
for good reason. The town is rich in history, and it is a
charming, friendly town, alive with activity—boating and

fishing in the summer months, skating and skiing and sledding in winter. Some of these activities I remember. We used to walk our sleds and skis to *les trois côtes*—the three hills. And I remember roller skating to the sounds of a Strauss waltz. Buildings that are interesting both aesthetically and architecturally comprise the neat, clean downtown. When I was nine we moved to a house on Rue Champlain, a short walk from the church in which I was baptized, beautiful Sainte-Agnès Catholic church, built in 1913, a neo-Gothic temple with a massive stained glass window behind the altar. Near the downtown marina is the tree-lined Veteran's Park where my parents would take us for walks.

I moved from my childhood home in Lac-Mégantic in 1952 when I was seventeen, though I have no solid recollection as to why. My sense (for most of the memories from my childhood are "sensed" rather than outright recalled) is that I simply wanted to get away from Lac-Mégantic, to get away from home.

I know, for one thing, that I was not doing well in school. I tried very hard and studied diligently but I had difficulty with concentration. I think I may have repeated the second grade but I cannot be sure as the memories of my time in grade school are very sketchy. I do remember specifically having difficulties with math in fourth grade. I was in a Catholic boarding school at the time, having been sent there with my sisters, the four of us removed from our home for reasons I did not (and would not, for years) understand. My teacher, Sister St. Joseph, kept sending me back to my seat to work out a particular problem I could not solve.

What she didn't tell me was that my math was correct; the error was grammatical—I'd failed to capitalize a word in my answer. It was at the end of the school year, probably late June, and it was warm and stuffy in the classroom, and I was tired. I felt that my nose was going to start to bleed and I asked to be excused and ran to the bathroom as the blood began to drip onto my uniform and the floor. I began to cry in frustration. It was not uncommon for me as a child to have nosebleeds during times of stress. An earlier day, in fact, sitting all alone in our living room, I had started out studying my catechism. We were supposed to know the answers by heart—word for word. It seemed that I had been working at it for hours. I repeated the questions and answers several times and then tried to answer the questions without looking. I could not do so and I became frustrated. Soon, I started to cry, feeling desperate, fearing that I would not be able to answer the questions the following day when the sister would ask them. I ended up with a severe nosebleed that day. And then, on the occasion in fourth grade with the math problem, the bleeding became so severe that the school had to call a doctor and then my parents. Sister St. Joseph silently prayed next to the bed and after everyone left, she cried and asked for my forgiveness.

With my grades suffering, I was, at some point, provided with a private tutor, the school inspector, Inspector Breton. Probably every two or three months, Inspector Breton would come to the convent to inspect the classes and the students' knowledge and note their progress. In the days leading up to his visit, everybody would be tense. The nuns were nervous and of course the students were, too. The school uniform was a black dress with a slim white collar, long beige stockings, and black shoes. We had to make sure for Inspector Breton's visits that our uniforms were freshly clean. When he'd knock on the door everyone would stand and say, "Bonjour Monsieur l'Inspector." He would walk in and we would not sit down until he told us to. Inspector Breton was tall and slim and balding and very stern. He never smiled. After we were again seated, he would walk around the classroom inspecting our desks. We were to sit straight with our feet flat on the floor and our hands on our desks. Then he would call names from a little notebook and question the students on different subjects.

Our family home was not far from Inspector Breton's and I think I walked by myself to his house for tutoring. I remember being alone in a room with him, probably his living room. The room was dark and scary to me. I quickly grew terrified and soon darted out of the house. I ran all the way home. It was the only attempt made to have Inspector Breton tutor me. Soon after that, we passed Inspector Breton's house in our car. It was just my father and me and I was in the backseat and I looked out and saw flames coming from the side entrance of Inspector Breton's house. I told my father who stopped the car immediately and backed up. He jumped out of the car and that's all I remember. I assume my father put the fire out or helped put it out. I don't know if Inspector Breton was home at the time, but it seemed curious to me that of all the houses in our town, the one that would catch fire would be the one that scared me so.

My family was musically inclined. My mother began adult life as a schoolteacher. One of my sisters and a few of my aunts and uncles were teachers as well. I think it was my mother who encouraged us all to learn music. There were six girls and six boys and we had a piano and we all played some kind of instrument or sang or did both. I remember taking a few piano lessons at the convent but had to stop because of the hard time I was having with my grades. But I loved music and enjoyed listening to opera on the gramophone. And I liked to sing, and had a good voice, my mother said. It was apparently a family trait; my oldest brothers sang in the church choir and my brother Jean was the lead singer. I remember singing as a little girl, at home, while rocking in a big rocking chair, and in my head late at night under the covers. I often sang a song about Jonah and the whale. Over and over I would sing it. "*Jonas dans la baleine disait je voudrais m'en aller, bo-boum bo-boum.*" Jonah in the whale, saying, "I want to go away..." It was comforting and soothing and in my bed I would imagine the whale swimming freely in the ocean, in calm warm waters, and I would imagine swimming with her, holding onto her fins, until I would finally fall asleep.

I was fragile and often ill. At age nine I had severe toothaches and was taken to the dentist where my front teeth were removed. On the chair I screamed and fought and clawed at the dentist as though my very life depended on it. My father had to hold me down and I fought even harder. Eventually I lost consciousness. At thirteen, I had toothaches again. I needed more teeth removed and this time I was taken to the hospital where they put me under ("I'll never go through that again," my father declared after the first time), but not before I fought in a similar way. It would be over thirty years before I would learn why both times I had lashed out the way I had.

I know that I did not finish eighth grade at the convent but was instead enrolled in a private school, *L'école Commerciale Desmarais*, to learn secretarial skills. I have a fuzzy recollection of my teacher and of learning shorthand, but my time at the commercial school did not prove especially productive. Ultimately, I went to work in a local hair salon where I learned hairdressing. Most likely, I was steered in that direction by my father, a Lac-Mégantic barber. It was a good decision for me, and I liked working with and learning from Madame Ruelle at her salon on Main Street in upper town.

My father's barber shop was not his only enterprise. He was an entrepreneur and in addition to the barber shop, he owned a restaurant, a pool room, and a bowling alley. Although I have no firsthand recollection of them doing so, my two oldest brothers, so I would be told years later by one of them, would go to work in the restaurant first thing every morning, rising early to wash dishes before school.

Father was well-respected around town. He was a self-made man, a man of little education (a severe asthmatic condition kept him out of school) but of high intelligence, at least according to my mother. He was popular and friendly and churchgoing and he doffed his hat to people on the sidewalk and everyone seemed to know him. And he was a good provider for his family, hard-working and responsible. He might have drunk too much at times. He might have had a violent temper at times. But that's not what I remembered about him. I remembered that my father was a good man.

After working in Madame Ruelle's hairdressing salon for about a year, I left Lac-Mégantic for a salon in Sherbrooke, a much larger city and a two-hour drive to the west, towards Montréal. I was seventeen. I know that my father drove me there because I can still see in my mind a glimpse of him in the living room of the owners of the salon, a woman and her husband, in whose home I would live for a time before eventually moving to a rooming house. Of the drive itself and the decision to move to Sherbrooke, I have no recollection.

The salon was in the center of the city at Rue King and Rue Wellington and I enjoyed working there. I was good as a hairdresser and in a short time, I built a clientele of patrons who would ask for me specifically. I liked Sherbrooke, and I liked my independence. I made friends and went out. I met Clement, a boy probably a couple years older than I, a great dancer and delightful to be with. He had an Indian motorcycle of which he was very proud, and I loved to climb on the backseat and go for rides with him. At one point there were six of us, three couples, and we would go on motorcycle rides on the weekends. We were young and alive and it was a wonderful year for me. One of the boys, nicknamed Bizou, was a mechanic and he drove a Harley Davidson. Bizou was tall with dark, curly hair and he was bold and adventurous. He broke up with one of the girls and asked me to be his girlfriend. I told him no—it would create hostility with the others, I said. It felt good that he asked me and I could tell he was hurt when I said no—most likely his pride more than his heart. But the group broke up anyway and I was sorry because I really liked Bizou. A few years later I would learn that he had been killed in a motorcycle accident.

One night in Sherbrooke, one of my girlfriends called, asking me to meet her for a burger. It was late and I was tired but she persuaded me anyway. At a diner, two older men began flirting with us. It was flattering. I was eighteen, but far less mature than even those years might suggest. I had little life experience, my friends were equally young, and I was trusting of everyone older than I. One of the men asked me for my phone number. His name was Aldéma and he was visiting Sherbrooke from Montréal, where he lived. Aldéma worked in construction and as a bartender. He was handsome, with a dark complexion and dark, curly hair, and a beautiful smile. He was thirty years old and I was smitten. I gave him my number and he called me a few days later and then came to visit from time to time. Very shortly we began to see more and more of each other. I quickly—naively— fell in love.

In 1954, having just turned nineteen, I moved to Montréal to live with Aldéma. We stayed in his sister's apartment on Barclay Avenue. I quickly found work in a hairdressing salon in downtown Montréal.

On Barclay Avenue one morning I saw a woman walking her dog—a beautiful, long-haired dog: an Afghan hound, I would later learn. I had a fear of dogs that went along with my other fears, typically forcing me to cross the street when I would see one coming my way, even a small dog. But there was something about this particular dog. He seemed gentle and I felt somehow unafraid as he passed by. Years later, the chance meeting with the dog would resonate with me greatly.

A year after moving to Montréal, Aldéma and I moved to Blind River, Ontario, five hundred miles from Montréal, close to seven hundred miles from Lac-Mégantic. It would be a pattern for Aldéma, who wouldn't, or couldn't, stay in the same place for very long. But deep inside I was grateful for the distance from home. Since I'd moved from Lac-Mégantic, I had rarely gone back. I felt obligated to return sometimes on holidays, to spend time with my father and mother and brothers and sisters, but I dreaded the trips. I would cry uncontrollably just thinking about returning home. I had no idea why.

In Blind River, I became pregnant, eventually giving birth to our son, Jacques. Aldéma's oldest sister Noëlla lived in Blind River as well and I could go to her anytime for help with my baby. Born a little over six pounds, Jacques was a delightful little doll, and a good baby, too. He hardly ever cried. I fussed over him and played with him. That he was a boy was a small disappointment for me at first, but the disappointment was short-lived. I was excited when he began to smile and then to hear him laugh. Thoughts I'd had of not wanting to have a baby evaporated quickly after Jacques was born. And I wanted my baby to have a good life.

Aldéma took a job tending bar at a small motel. There

was a main house where the owners lived that had a large dance hall with a bar where the people of the small town would gather. The rest of the motel consisted of eight cabins, one of which the owners gave us to use in exchange for Aldéma's employment in the bar. We moved to a larger cabin after Jacques was born. It had one bedroom and a large kitchen.

One snowy day Aldéma and I were in our cabin when I heard a commotion outside. I looked through the frosted window and saw a violent fight of some kind, with a man standing over someone—another man or a woman, I could not tell which—swinging his fists and beating this person as he or she lay in the snow. The next thing I remember Aldéma was helping me off the floor. The scene outside had made me faint, though it seemed very strange that it would do so, that it would have such an effect on me to where I would lose consciousness. I don't know what became of the people outside. I imagine the fight was eventually broken up, and maybe the police were called or maybe they were not. I don't remember anything more about it. But it stuck with me for some reason, as did similar incidents, each of them filling me with unexplained anxiety.

Soon after moving to Blind River, Aldéma began to drink very heavily. Or maybe there were signs that he was an alcoholic all along and I just missed them. Either way, the alcohol changed him, fueling his temper; he would go into rages and outbursts, throwing and breaking things (not unlike, as I would be told years later, my father when he drank heavily). For a short time prior to finding the bartending job at the motel, we'd lived in an old, sparsely furnished country house. We had an orange tabby cat and, in a fury one day, Aldéma kicked the cat across the living room. In fear, I ran out of the house. I kept running, to where I had no idea. I just wanted to get away. Aldéma followed and soon caught up with me and took me back home. He apologized.

Aldéma's friends in Blind River were other bartenders, and heavy drinkers and bootleggers and even pimps. I don't know how he came to know them all but the associations Aldéma made distressed me. And he cheated on me, too, I was certain of it. Aldéma was a womanizer, often flirting openly in my presence. But the worst was the temper. Although he never hit me, the potential for violence seemed palpable and I was constantly afraid. I was small—just five feet two and a little over a hundred pounds. In 1956, I took Jacques and left, moving back to Montréal.

I had called my parents, and my father and my oldest brother Jean met me at a motel when I arrived in Montréal. "I think it would be a good idea, Marcelle, if you were to find a home for the baby while you come home and decide what you want to do," my father told me. "I've contacted a facility for you."

"What kind of facility?" I asked.

"It's a place where they care for young children, sometimes placing them in private homes. Jacques will be well taken care of." Though he didn't state it outright, I knew that bringing Jacques—a child born out of wedlock—to Lac-Mégantic would be unacceptable. And I knew, on some level, that the facility—an orphanage, in reality—was probably best for Jacques. I knew I lacked the maturity to be the mother I needed to be. Yet the exact details of sending Jacques away, even of saying goodbye to him, remain hazy to this day. Did Jean and his wife, who would later adopt three children, consider adopting Jacques? I cannot be certain.

Though my father had already contacted the couple who owned the salon in Sherbrooke so I could take my old job back and finish my hairdressing course (his ultimate plan was to have me come back to work in his Lac-Mégantic salon), I decided to stay in Montréal. I had enough money to rent a small room, nothing more really than a bedroom with a hotplate, but it was enough for me and I soon found an opening at a nearby salon where I started working.

Shortly after moving to Montréal, however, I discovered I was pregnant again, or thought that I was, the result of my last intimate night with Aldéma in Blind River. I wanted nothing more to do with Aldéma and I couldn't, on my own, even handle the one child that I had. There were pills in those days, although they were, of course, illegal, and I managed to get my hands on some. I had no idea what to expect. I began hemorrhaging soon after taking them. I was working and I had to take a cab home, where I passed out in the hallway of the rooming house. When I came to, I had no idea where I was. A loud *tick...tick...tick* boomed in my ears. It was an alarm clock on the night table next to the bed I found myself lying in. The bedroom was that of the house's owners who had found me unconscious in the hallway.

Two police officers were standing next to the bed.

"Where did you get the pills, Miss Drouin?" one of the officers asked.

"I don't know the name of the person. And I don't know where she lives."

"You must understand the importance, Miss Drouin. Where did you get the pills?" he repeated.

"I don't know." I was weak and I was scared. These were the days when women died from back alley abortions and if we did not die we could go to jail. I wondered if they would take me in, imprison me and force me to tell them what they wanted to know. But the officers must have sensed I could be of no help to them and eventually they went away.

A doctor I saw soon after that said that I had not been pregnant. "You went through all this for no reason," he told me.

Suddenly I missed my baby terribly and I cried out for him. I was now all alone. And probably out of a job as well. I called my sister asking for advice, telling her how desperate I felt, and she in turn called Aldéma's sister. Soon Aldéma showed up in Montréal, repentant. He made promises. "We'll get Jacques back, and things will be different," he said. I believed him. We took Jacques out of the orphanage and moved back in with Aldéma's sister for a short time. In May of 1957, we were married. I was four months pregnant with our second son, Serge.

Soon after Serge was born, we moved back to Blind River, to a house out in the country. The house was nice and almost new, but too far out into the country for my comfort.

I was terrified of being alone at night. I hated the remoteness of our house and I hated the darkness. Aldéma would often go out at night and it would just be the children and me at home. Aldéma would be bartending, or maybe out with the same people he'd hooked up with before, the drinking buddies and the bootleggers. Aldéma himself was bootlegging by then. Or maybe he'd be with a woman. I would lie awake long into the night, hearing every sound, every creak. I'd often sleep with a knife under my pillow for protection. I could never say what it was, exactly, I was fearful of, and why I felt the need to have the knife. I just knew that somehow I felt more secure with it there, under my pillow, quickly and easily accessible.

In 1958, I became pregnant with our third son, Alain. On a September day that year, two police officers came to our house, telling me that it was imperative that I get in touch with my brother Jean back in Lac-Mégantic. My family was looking for me. I was very pregnant and I saw them looking at each other and then one of the officers stepped back to where Aldéma was standing and the two talked in hushed tones. The other officer turned towards me. "We received a call from your family. They've been unable to reach you. It's urgent that you call your brother." There was bad news from home and I began to shake and I wanted the officers to go away. When they did finally leave, Aldéma told me to call my brother. But we didn't have a phone yet in the house and I didn't go out looking for one. Nor did I ask Aldéma what the other police officer had told him. I didn't want to know anything about the bad news from home, even though—or maybe because—I had a sense of what it was.

Sometime later that day I was driving to the drugstore to pick up some things. The radio was on in the car, but very low. I heard a news report about a murder in the province of Quebec. If they gave the name of the victim, I didn't hear it. Quebec is a large province and the name could not have meant a thing to me. But then I pulled into the drugstore and as I paid the cashier for my purchase, my eyes fell upon the stack of newspapers on the lower shelves to the left of where I was standing. On the front page was a picture of my father. The headline: *Patricide in Mégantic.*

Shaking and dazed, I picked up the newspaper, paid for it, and walked out of the store. I don't remember driving home or much else about that day or the days shortly thereafter. Because it was late in my pregnancy my doctor advised me against driving the distance and I felt relief that I had an excuse not to travel the seven hundred miles to my father's funeral.

A few months later, my sister Louise came to visit. When we were alone she told me what had happened. It was a late September morning. Father had driven my brother Philippe to the family's summer chalet to gather some vegetables from the garden. It was a good-sized property and so was the garden. Father went to work at his downtown barber shop. When he and Philippe did not come home for dinner that night my mother sent Louise and my brother Louis to the chalet. My father's car was not there. The electricity had been turned off for the winter and Louise and Louis made their way around with only a flashlight. Louise started to go up the steps and tripped over my father's body. Of Philippe, there were no signs.

Frightened, they drove to the police station and found the staff there in an uproar. Earlier that same day a provincial policeman had been killed while attempting to arrest a man suspected of murder, rape, and the mutilation of a body. For this small town police department, where most offenses they handled were no more serious than maybe breaking up a weekend fight between drunks, two murders on the same day were overwhelming.

After my brother shot my father he took off in my father's car. An inexperienced driver, he drove around aimlessly before ultimately running the car off the road and getting it stuck. He hitchhiked to Montréal where he was found three days later and detained. Eventually, he'd be sentenced to fifteen years.

Hearing from Louise the story of my father's death did something to my deepest inner self. I did not know how to grieve for my father. The feelings I had were foreign and disorienting. I was twenty-three, with three young children and I was unable to deal with both the death of my father and with feelings conjured up by his death. Distant, hidden memories. Louise's telling of the incident went out of my conscious mind. I never told anyone. In time, my memories of Louise's story simply disappeared.

CHAPTER TWO

Things Forgotten

~

As for my childhood in Lac-Mégantic, I probably would have remembered much more but my role, for reasons I would not understand until much later, was to forget, to not think of the past. Still, I never knew when a memory would pop up out of seemingly nowhere. It happens still. Sometimes as I write, or read, or talk to someone. Or watch a movie. You hear something, but it's only later that you realize what you heard caused a flashback. It's all a part of having repressed memories.

Alain, my third son, was born November 11, 1958, less than two months after his grandfather was killed. I remember, just before giving birth, telling the nurse about my father's death.

"Oh, how did he die?" she asked.

"He was shot," I replied.

"Oh…I'm so sorry," she said. "Was it a hunting accident?" Murders were rare in Canada then. Hunting accident would have been a reasonable guess.

"Yes," I said, "it was a hunting accident."

In truth, there was no room for thoughts about shootings. Or funerals, either. Or murder trials. With three boys, more than I could handle, I was overwhelmed, near a breaking point. Lac-Mégantic was hundreds of miles away. It might as well have been a million. If I felt any sense of loss, it was not noticeable to me. My childhood had been lost long ago and things and people—people like my father—who represented my childhood were already gone. I was in Blind River now, a wife and mother with an entirely different life. What was Lac-Mégantic to me?

Close to a year went by. On October 27, 1959, I was in Elliott Lake, Ontario, a small town not far from Blind River. I was in a Catholic hospital about to give birth to my fourth son, Daniel. I was lying on the birthing bed, waiting for the doctor, covered by a sheet, my legs restrained, labor contractions close together. A nun came into the room to see how I was doing and settled into a chair right next to the bed. Something snapped inside of me the moment she sat down. I began to scream and I tried to get up and jump off the bed. The nun held me down and I fought her. "Mrs. Guy, stop it!" she said. I'm certain she must have thought my reaction was from labor pains. "You'll hurt the baby! Mrs. Guy! *Please.*" I kept fighting, flailing my arms wildly trying to get free. Every fiber of my being wanted to get away, although, if I had been forced to explain why, I could not have said.

The doctor came in just then and took over from the nun and I eventually calmed down. Daniel was born very shortly thereafter in an otherwise unremarkable delivery.

The incident bothered me for years to come, and for years to come I would remain at a total loss as to why I had reacted as I had.

Life with Aldéma, meanwhile, was getting worse. The place we were living in at the time, all six of us, was a small cabin—more of a shack than a house, with a single bedroom and a tiny kitchen. Our chief means of support was Aldéma's bootlegging. Alcohol was very tightly regulated by the Liquor Control Board of Ontario. Aldéma sold it, illegally, out of our cabin and people came and went at all hours. I had no idea who they were but I was terrified of all the drunkards and I was ashamed of our way of living. Aldéma's own drinking was getting worse, and so was his temper. In rages, he would storm around the cabin, kicking and throwing things.

In March of 1960, an undercover detective came by the cabin and bought a case of beer from Aldéma, paying for it with a marked twenty-dollar bill. Shortly afterwards, there was a loud knock at the door. With my baby in my arms, I opened the door and four cops in uniform came crashing in, searching for the marked bill. It would provide the evidence they needed. Aldéma was taken off to jail. I felt relief. It was an opportunity for me to leave. I was near a breakdown. I had friends from the church and I consulted with them. I wanted to go back to Montréal but I was too tired and confused to think it through. The kids and I stayed at my friends' house for a while and they helped me plan our future. Aldéma's sister and niece from Montréal came and took the boys and I stayed behind a few weeks to rest and figure out what to do. The children were now safe and I used the time to clear my head of the nightmare we'd been living. The break was extremely helpful and I was grateful for my friends.

Finally, I secured some temporary accommodations from the Catholic Church in Montréal and shortly I was back there, reunited with my boys. Then, with governmental assistance, I moved us into a small apartment and eventually took on work as a waitress, first at a nearby delicatessen and later at the upscale Monterrey Restaurant on Rue Sainte-Catherine. The apartment building we lived in was full of young families and the neighbors would often watch the boys while I worked, as I would often watch their children when they were off working. I tried to be a good mother to my children. It was not always easy, but I knew it was a much better life than what we had in Ontario with Aldéma.

But Aldéma, out of jail after a few months, followed me back to Montréal, trying to get us back together, making promises again. He would enlist his sister to come talk to me, too. This went on for a year or so. I would have none of it. Aldéma eventually gave up and then disappeared from my life, but I would remain married to him for some time to come. In Canada in those days divorce required a provable charge of infidelity. Aldéma was unfaithful. But I had no proof.

Meanwhile, I met a man, Wendel Eatman. Wendel was

younger than I, attractive and athletic. He was just nineteen, but he looked older. Wendel lived a few buildings from ours and we crossed paths sometimes on the street or at the park where I would take the boys to play. One time, he saw us on the way to the park and he took one of the boys' hands and we walked to the park together where I watched as he played with the boys, pushing their swings and helping them up the slides. And it dawned on me that Aldéma had never taken the boys out to play; they'd never had a male figure take them to a park. Wendel looked so natural playing with the boys and they had such a fun time.

We walked home together and Wendel asked me for a date. I was puzzled. I didn't think of myself as attractive, and there I was with four kids. I said yes, and we went out a couple of times—a movie, a walk. Then one evening, we decided to go to a nearby club where we danced and drank. Aldéma never danced and it had been so long since I had danced in the arms of a man and it felt good, it felt warm. I got caught up in the spirit of the evening and drank more than usual. I hadn't a great tolerance for alcohol to begin with. At the end of the night, I went with Wendel back to his place without hesitation.

Strange the things we remember. Wendel turned the lights on in the kitchen as we walked into his apartment and the first thing I saw were a couple cockroaches scurrying away on the kitchen counter. Even in my buzzed head, the sight alarmed me and I should have left. I was terrified of the crawling pests. The kitchen was clean otherwise, and scarcely furnished.

I slept with Wendel. And then sometime later that night, Wendel's roommate forced himself upon me. Afterwards, I left the apartment disgusted with myself, realizing why Wendel had been interested in me. I'd begun having feelings for Wendel but for him I was an easy target. I was disappointed. In Wendel. In myself. I was angry with myself for being so naïve. And I was angry with Wendel and his roommate for violating my body and whatever hopes I had had for Wendel and me. I promised never to drink again, a promise I have kept ever since.

Several months later I read in the paper that Wendel's roommate had been sitting in a movie theater when another man, a virtual stranger, perhaps just another theater customer, shot him in the head. No real reason was ever uncovered. Deep inside I felt strange about it. What exactly I felt, I did not know. But years from then I would have cause to wonder at the implications of the shooting. I would think about Inspector Breton's house catching on fire. And I would think about my father.

Wendel, in the meantime, would not leave me alone. I wanted nothing more to do with him but he would come to see me constantly. He would stalk me, dropping by my apartment at all hours and stopping by the restaurant while I was working. It became disturbing, and then frightening, so much so that I was forced to move to another place. Wendel found me. One night, with the boys at a neighbor's, I came home to find Wendel hiding under my bed. I ran out of the apartment and called the police but he was gone by the time they arrived. The close brush with the police must have been enough to scare Wendel off because I never saw him again.

The strange experience intensified my sense of being overwhelmed. It was all a lot to take; too much, really. I was working long hours and raising four small boys by myself. They were beautiful to me and I wanted the best for them. But I worried about them constantly, feeling ill-equipped to handle the responsibility of taking care of them. Sometimes I became so overwhelmed that I would call a city counselor and ask to have the boys put in a foster home, just for a few days, just so I could get a break and get myself together. I knew it was either that or give up the boys entirely. The counselors understood.

I often felt alone, especially at night when the children were sleeping. And I was afraid, too, even with the kids in the house—afraid of the dark, afraid of someone breaking in. One night I could hear the neighbors fighting loudly next door. It was so frightening to me that I barricaded the door and sat in the middle of my bed all night, afraid that someone would force their way in and beat me or worse. When daylight finally came, I fell asleep but I soon had to get up and get the kids ready for school.

I was still legally married to Aldéma and I yearned for a close relationship with a decent man, someone to be close to, to confide in. Maybe even a father for the boys. I wanted a normal life for my family. Stability. I wanted to not be afraid anymore. I was becoming melancholic. Is it any wonder that I had no time, or energy, to devote to the past— any wonder that things forgotten stayed forgotten?

CHAPTER THREE
Running Still

~

I WANTED TO RUN AWAY. I WAS WEIGHED DOWN BY LIFE and frequently depressed. What I didn't know at the time was that I was looking to run away from more than just my circumstances—having to raise the boys myself, the aloneness, the vague fears. I wanted to run—was running still, in fact—from Lac-Mégantic. The prospect of returning for holidays still filled me with unexplained dread, which in turn led to a sense of guilt for feeling the dread. Even in Montréal I was still too close. I didn't ever want to return, but I had no decent excuse not to.

I suppose it was this that made my eyes stop at a personal ad in an English language newspaper I was browsing one morning. It must have been, for I had never looked at such ads before, or at least not seriously enough to where I would have considered answering one, and I can think of no other reason why this particular ad should have caught my interest. The man had his qualities, to be certain. He described himself as serious and stable. He was a nondrinker and nonsmoker. He seemed, in other words, not at all like Aldéma and that in and of itself would have made him attractive to me. But there was something more. The man was an American. He was from another country. From somewhere else in the world where I could not imagine they had probably ever heard of Lac-Mégantic. This may have been the thing that attracted me the most, although I would not have consciously understood so then. But looking back, it was as if there was a force inside me, guiding me.

I put the ad aside but a few days later curiosity got the better of me and I wrote to the address in the ad. James wrote back. He was from the Philadelphia, Pennsylvania area, the borough of Yeadon. He had his own house there and a good job working for the Federal Government. He was also a black man, but this did not matter to me. This was in early 1963 but race was not the incendiary issue in Canada that it was starting to become in the U.S. at that time. The African-Canadian population was very small. I remember someone joking, "Yes, Canada treats its African citizens very well. All five of them."

In fact, it wouldn't be until fifth grade that I would see a black man for the first time. He was a Catholic priest who had come straight from Africa. He was traveling from school to school to speak about African children. I thought he was beautiful—very dark with brilliant white teeth, and he spoke French with an accent. The nuns hung a poster in the class-room. The goal was to convert little African children to

Catholicism so they could go to heaven. At the bottom of the poster were several steps that led up to the top which was heaven. On the lowest step was a picture of a child glued to a toothpick and as we gave money, the child was moved up the steps. Everyone in our class got involved. I collected all the pennies I could find and took them to school and we were all so excited to think we could save at least one little African child from hell or from purgatory.

James and I kept writing and then exchanged phone numbers and soon we were talking quite often. We spoke on the phone at least once or twice a week for months. He had vacation time around Christmas and he planned a visit. I looked forward to meeting him but I felt uneasy, too. I even thought briefly of severing the relationship. I wondered what I was getting myself into. I had to think of the boys, too. I didn't want to expose them to any potential harm. But in the end, I decided to let James come.

In November, I was sitting in my doctor's office when a call came in from the doctor's wife. He picked up the phone and became very serious as his wife told him the news that he would subsequently share with me: President Kennedy had been shot. Kennedy had been popular in Canada, with a charismatic personality that reached across the border. Too, he was Catholic, the first to be elected President of the United States. That made all of us Catholics, especially my mother, as I recall, admiring fans of his. The news of the assassination was heartbreaking and I felt a deep hurt inside. It stayed with me for weeks, longer perhaps than it should have. But that's the way certain things would affect me; they would sink me into days of sadness, sometimes intensely so.

James arrived a few days before Christmas and I met him at the train station. He was average looking, with a small mustache and glasses, but trim and neat, and after the initial awkwardness, we got along very well. He stayed for a week and we promised to keep in close contact.

We took things slowly, but the relationship progressed. Over the next few years, James would visit several times and we would talk on the phone at least once a week. He was conservative, a serious man, quiet and soft spoken. I felt no violence in him and that was crucial for me. The boys liked him a great deal. When he came he always brought gifts and he would take us all out to the movies. Not overly demonstrative, he would nonetheless show me affection, holding my hand when we walked downtown or putting his arm around my waist. I liked James very much. I suppose I learned to love him.

In time we began talking about marriage. James began to inquire about positions in Montréal, perhaps a U.S. government job at the Embassy. But he could find nothing. It didn't help that he knew no French. And there was another problem; I was still legally married to Aldéma. We talked about the kids and me moving to Yeadon instead of him moving to Montréal. He could keep his job and perhaps the divorce would be easier to obtain in the States. It was a hard decision. I was afraid. Would I be doing the right thing? Moving all of us out of Canada was a big step. But in some ways I was drowning and I imagined that if I stayed in Montréal alone, I would eventually lose the boys.

They needed a father in their lives.

I went to visit James for a couple of weeks in early1967, leaving the kids with my mother. I wanted to know that James's world was the right place to move us. I wanted to give my boys a normal family life. It was all I really wanted. Normalcy. James's home had a lot to recommend it. It had James, of course—stable and secure. He lived in a duplex that he owned, a tidy three-bedroom unit in a quiet neighborhood. It was a white neighborhood, James, in fact, having been the first black to move into it. Schools were close, and churches. It would be a good place for the boys. And I learned that the move would indeed provide an easier route to a divorce. In Canada I had to prove infidelity, but it would be sufficient in the States to file for desertion. And I know now that Yeadon provided something else I was searching for: more distance from Lac-Mégantic.

James and I went to an attorney in Philadelphia where we were advised that I needed to be living in the United States for six months before I could do much of anything in so far as proceeding with the divorce. The attorney recommended I cross the border with my sons as visitors only. "If you look like you're crossing with a more permanent intent," he warned, "and you don't have the necessary paperwork, you'll be turned away." This is exactly what happened when I attempted to enter a month later at Champlain in a car James had bought for us. It was the four boys and me and all of our worldly possessions. Apparently we looked nothing like tourists. We looked like a family that had every intention of staying forever and we were denied entry.

I dropped off a good portion of our things at my sister's house and the next morning I nervously drove us to a different crossing and we made it through without a problem.

I was excited to be in a new place, but once we settled in, James became different somehow. Always quiet, he was now more distant, even aloof. Some of it I attributed to his inexperience with women. His first day off to work, just after we had moved into his home, he gave me a list of household chores that he needed to have done. I felt more like a maid than a lover. I felt disappointment.

Soon, I came to realize that some of his distance was a reaction to the times and place in which we lived. We were a mixed couple, not a popular thing to be, and James often would go out of his way to keep us from looking like a couple in public. The handholding ceased. He stopped putting his arm around my shoulders or waist when in public. I felt like an outcast. We'd often walk a few steps apart. I picked him up once after an office softball game and was disturbed to see him look away from me as I drove up, pretending not to see me. I passed by him to find a place to park. He was walking with some coworkers and he waited until they were out of sight before turning around and walking back to the car.

Not that the racism wasn't real. I had seen it myself. There was the woman who wouldn't slide over to allow James and me to sit down in the church pew the first Sunday, the only Sunday, we attended mass together. She looked at us—a black man with a white woman—with complete disdain. It would turn out to be the last time I would attend Sunday mass. Then one morning very soon after moving in, I opened our front door to see the porch littered with dog bones. I tried to brush it off, thinking someone had the wrong house; we didn't have a dog. But the message was clear. We were dogs. Not long after, at the A&P, a cashier turned to another cashier and said loudly, so that I could hear, "I didn't know we allowed dogs in here." This made them both laugh. Once at school, Alain, only about nine, was cornered by a gang of bullies who punched him repeatedly while saying things like, "Your mother is a nigger lover. Are you a nigger lover?" The boys made good friends at school and they didn't always tell me what was going on. But this time, Alain had come home vomiting and he told me what happened. I went to the police to file a report. Alain knew the names of the other kids. One, as it happened, was the police chief's son and nothing ever happened to the kids. But at least Alain wasn't bothered again.

We stayed, the boys and I. I had my visa renewed and we stayed. James and I weren't as close as I would have liked, but he was reliable and for that I was appreciative. He provided us with the security I needed. And the distance from home as well.

In 1968, I experienced the sadness of a Kennedy killing again, only this time it was much worse for me. I cried for several days after Bobby Kennedy was assassinated. I drove to Media, Pennsylvania with Alain and Daniel to see the funeral train that took his body to Washington D.C. for burial at Arlington. A million people lined the tracks between New York and Washington. I broke down as the train passed, crying uncontrollably, dropping to my knees. I didn't know what was wrong with me. I knew my reaction was disproportionate. I was like a raw nerve and I never knew what might inflame me.

Later that year I secured a permanent visa and in December of 1968, I was officially divorced from Aldéma. Just days later, James and I were married. It was important to him to have the marriage take place before the end of the year. The kids and I were now dependents, a write-off for James for the 1968 tax year. The wedding consisted of me and James and the minister and we were married in the minister's office. I wore an attractive checkered suit that James approved of, though he gave me a thumbs-down for my choice of earrings. James was always well dressed and everything matched. After we exchanged vows, we went straight home.

The marriage was disappointing but I made the best of it. Our moments of intimacy were few and far between and largely unsatisfying, but James sincerely loved the kids. "The thing that would hurt me the most," he once told me, "is if the boys didn't think of me as their father." But one time I came home to find him threatening to use his belt on Danny. They were in the basement. I don't know; maybe Danny deserved punishment. I was not against disciplining the kids. But there was something about the thought of seeing the boys being hit. Something very distressing. I lashed out. "You are never to punish the children!" I yelled at James. In my presence, he never again would but I would learn years later that the belt came out from time to time when I was not in the house.

I went to work at a downtown Philadelphia restaurant where big cockroaches walked everywhere—on the counters, the walls, the floor. The staff had to keep personal items in the basement and I was afraid of going down there. I didn't work there long. Next, I worked for a year or so at the upscale Scott Moss Restaurant where I made a few good friends but witnessed a lot of bigotry. Then, I went to work, first as a waitress and later a hostess, in a Holiday Inn. There, a young, handsome police officer came in for coffee from time to time. Julian was friendly and we'd talk and I liked the way he looked in his uniform. Often he came in during his breaks with a book and notebook and I learned he was going back to college to try to improve his chances for advancement in the police force. Over time our conversations became more flirtatious. One evening I was at the front desk getting some information for a customer when I felt a hand on my shoulder. I turned and it was Julian.

"Did you get a promotion?" he asked.

I smiled. "I'll be back in the dining room in a few minutes if you'd like to wait."

"Sure." Back in the dining room, Julian asked me what time my shift ended. "I was thinking maybe we could go for a cup of coffee. Maybe meet at the Marriott across the street?"

There was an emptiness in my life that James, in his reserved, almost sedate way, was unable to fill. Julian was caring and affectionate and sensitive. The affair lasted six months. It was passionate, it was loving. We both knew it would go no further. Nothing was ever said, but we knew. James was important in my life and to the kids. He gave us the secure, solid life that I wanted for them and the father figure they needed. I struggled with the affair and decided to end it before it ruined everyone's life. Nobody ever found out about the affair, but I would always hold on to the memories of Julian and of those six months.

In the meantime, James and I, both perhaps sensing that a change would do us good, began talking about moving. It could be a new start of sorts. The idea appealed to me greatly and I encouraged James to see about a transfer to another state. Even farther away from Lac-Mégantic. It was not enough to be in another country. We needed to move to the other side of it. In 1973, James put in for a transfer to California, 3,500 miles away from my home town.

I was running still.

CHAPTER FOUR
At the Chalet

~

JAMES'S TRANSFER WAS APPROVED. WE'D BE MOVING TO San Francisco. He flew out first while the kids and I waited for the school year to end. In San Mateo, James found us a little three-bedroom furnished bungalow for rent. But as the time approached for us to join him, I began having second thoughts. School ended but I procrastinated. I had made friends in Pennsylvania. So had the kids. And a coworker at the Holiday Inn warned me about California. It had something of a reputation in the early '70s. "Drugs, Elle," she said. "You'll have to watch that your boys don't start doing drugs." And of course there was Julian. It would mean the end for Julian and me.

James kept calling from San Mateo, losing patience, wondering why we weren't coming. Finally, I could put it off no longer. I knew there was no turning back. We boxed everything up and loaded our Kingswood Estate station wagon and began the long trek west, made much longer by my decision to drive northeast first, to Lac-Mégantic, to say goodbye to my mother and brothers and sisters. That leg of the trip might have been responsible for some of the ambivalence about the move. Saying goodbye to my mother and brothers and sisters was difficult. There was no telling when I'd ever come back. Perhaps never.

Probably the ambivalence was also a reflection of my general mood. The idea of change, even potentially good change, was stressful for me. It was a confusing time and I was still something of a raw nerve, reacting to seemingly tiny things in ways that were surprising even to myself. Whole days would sometimes be filled with anxiety. I listened to music, which always seemed to be able to change my moods. "Jesus Christ Superstar" had been released just a year prior and I could not stop listening to it. Some of the lyrics resonated with me intensely, though I did not know why. "I don't know how to love him," the character of Judas sang before his death. *Does he love me, too? Does he care for me?* And then the line that mysteriously pierced through me: *You have murdered me…you have murdered me…*

Sometimes the picture would come into my head. The little girl on the bed, a nun sitting beside her. The girl was still and lifeless, her arms stretched out above her head, her hands tied to the headboard, prayer candles upside down and placed on her chest. The image, like a flashback had always followed me everywhere I went. I didn't know where it came from or why it followed me, but I never questioned it. Somehow I knew I couldn't, as though exploring the image was forbidden. I accepted it as just a part of me, a natural part, like a scar on my arm or the color of my hair. I moved from one ocean to another and still the image followed. The little girl. Eventually, she became the only link remaining to Lac-Mégantic.

When we arrived in Lac-Mégantic to visit, we didn't stay for long. I said goodbye to my mother who promised to come and visit. I said goodbye to my brothers and sisters and we headed toward Montréal, where other members of my family lived and I said goodbye to them, too, calling them on the phone rather than visiting with them. California was a long way away and we needed to get ourselves on the road.

From Montréal, we headed west across Canada and my heart suddenly felt lighter and California seemed to beckon from the distance and life felt exciting and new. The boys felt it, too, and the trip became cheerful and fun. I loved being out on the road with the boys. We took in the scenery. We saw a moose cross the road right in from of us. We got nervous as I navigated the narrow roads that ran along the cliffs of the Canadian Rockies and then we later laughed at our nervousness. Each night we stopped at Holiday Inns when possible; I could get a discount since I worked for them and the kids enjoyed jumping in the swimming pools at the end of each long day. We drove to Vancouver and then headed south through Washington and Oregon and then ultimately California. Oddly, it became colder the farther south we went and somewhere just before the Golden Gate Bridge I switched the car's air conditioning off and turned on the heater.

We arrived in San Mateo and right away I liked the house that James had rented for us. It was small, but it was comfortable. It had three bedrooms and James and I took one and the boys paired off and took the others. The kitchen shared a fireplace with the living room and also had a pass through counter that I particularly liked. The living room had a sliding glass door that opened to a small backyard. The neighborhood was clean and quiet. We settled in. The boys started school in the fall and they made friends quickly.

Julian came out to visit once. He had been sent to Nevada for training and called and said he wanted to see me once more. He flew to San Francisco for the day. James was at work and the kids were at school and Julian and I went for a drive.

"I've never been across the Golden Gate Bridge," Julian said. "And I'd like to cross it with you." We drove across the Golden Gate and then along the Redwood Highway through Sausalito and up to Mill Valley. We stopped along the way, strolled on a pier and held hands and looked out at the water. We didn't say much. At the end of the day I drove him back to the airport and we embraced and kissed and he walked towards his gate and I watched as his plane took off. I never saw him again.

~

AFTER A FEW WEEKS OF LIVING IN SAN MATEO, I took a job at the airport, as a cashier and hostess with Host International. On weekends, James and the kids and I explored San

Mateo and the surrounding area. Driving towards San Jose one day we passed a horseback riding stable offering trail rides. I mentioned the stable to a friend at work and we went one day. The trail was woodsy and beautiful and I immersed myself in the tranquility. I loved the pace and feel of the horse and shortly thereafter I began to take riding lessons. Eventually I was able to ride the two-mile trail by myself with an older horse named Rocky.

Rocky was a gentle horse who knew the routine and followed the trail without any guidance. Almost every weekend I'd arrive at the stables and brush Rocky and saddle him and we would ride. Rocky would lope in easy, long, smooth strides and my hair would flow behind me and I would feel as though I was flying...floating...dreaming. It was just Rocky and me and the sylvan trees and the dappled sunshine and the cool air and the warm earth. Neil Diamond would echo in my mind: *Ride, come on baby, ride...Let me make your dreams come true...*

All too quickly we'd be back at the stables. I'd caress Rocky's neck and promise him I'd be back soon and walk to my car. I'd sit for a minute or two in the driver's seat, half disoriented, trying to place myself, ultimately coming to the realization that I had to drive home, that I had to face the real world, that I had to surrender the blissful freedom I had found in the woods. I wanted to cry at the sense of loss. It wasn't as if Rocky wouldn't be there for me the following weekend, but there was a sense in those days of something imminent, something looming. I had no idea what it was, but whatever it was, I knew my weekend escapes on Rocky weren't going to be able to keep me from it, or it from me.

We stayed in San Mateo for a year and then decided we needed to buy a bigger house. We looked for homes around the Bay area but everything was either too small or far too expensive and eventually we settled on a house in Petaluma, about an hour's drive north of San Francisco. It was much bigger than our house in San Mateo. A tri-level with four bedrooms and three baths with a large family room and a large kitchen. I rode one more time before we moved and said goodbye to Rocky.

James made the commute into the city every day from Petaluma and I decided to commute, too. Host International had offered me a promotion and I went to work in the accounting office. The offer was too good to pass up even though the distance meant getting up every morning at 4:30. I liked the work and I liked my boss and co-workers.

In September of that year, 1975, my mother came to visit for two weeks, flying out all by herself. I thought it was brave of her, an older woman who didn't speak the language. As for me, I felt anxious in the days leading up to her arrival, again without knowing why. I took off from work for the two weeks and we had fun with the boys and we spent our time driving along the coast and seeing the sights of San Francisco. One day we drove down to Los Angeles where James happened to be taking a training class for a couple of weeks. We stayed overnight and the three of us did some sightseeing and took a tour of Hollywood. We snapped pictures of everything and bought souvenirs and visited Universal Studios. My mother had a good time and her visit was a nice one for us both. But I felt the barrier between us. As had been the pattern in our family, conversations were cautiously selected. No one spoke of certain things. I often wondered if she, too, felt the partition between us. The anxiety didn't go away until she left.

By this time, other things were building that would change my life. I was always proud of my well-mannered children. They were polite and respectful wherever we went, but during Mother's visit, I found myself shocked when one of them argued with me, cursing at me right in front of my mother. And I remembered my friend warning me about drugs in California. Was it possible?

Then, when I went back to work, I found my boss had been promoted. We had a new controller. Slim with light brown hair, Paul was young, maybe late twenties. He introduced himself and coolly welcomed me back from my vacation. Right away, I sensed something negative about him. The office was quiet and my co-workers looked tense. When Paul momentarily left the office, one of the bookkeepers filled me in. Paul was intending to change the way things had been done in the office. All of our jobs were on the line. "He's changing the routine for no reason at all. Except, I guess, just to display his authority," she said.

Over the course of the next few days, I could feel that the mood of the office had drastically changed. Everybody felt it. Work became a stressful place and it was hard for me to hide my feelings about Paul. I didn't like him. One day the company altered the dress code, allowing for women to wear pants. I said it was about time. Paul preferred that the women in "his" office remain in skirts. A couple of weeks later, I arrived at work in dress pants.

"Your outfit is inappropriate," Paul said to me in front of everybody.

"It's consistent with the dress code," I replied. I felt suddenly tense and I felt embarrassed that he called me out in front of everybody.

"Yes," he said, "the dress code says you can wear pants, but it also stipulates that an employee's manner of dress must be 'appropriate'. That's inappropriate."

"Why? I don't think so." I felt myself trembling slightly.

"Well. Let's see what the manager has to say."

Paul set up a time for us to see the manager. The assistant manager was there, too. Both agreed my pants were fine. "What, in particular, do you think is wrong with Marcelle's outfit?" asked Vivian, the assistant manager.

"Oh…nothing," said Paul. "I just wanted to make sure."

I left work early that day, crying as I drove home. For some reason the embarrassment bothered me very deeply. I told James about the incident, but he didn't have much to offer. He worked for a large, union-protected company. "Ignore him," he suggested. *He's my manager!* I wanted to yell back at him. *How can I ignore him?* We were in bed and James rolled over and I felt alone. I wanted to scream and strike back at someone. I sat on my side of the bed with my head in my hands and I slowly ran my fingernails down the sides of my face feeling the burn as blood dripped down. "I hate you," I whispered to myself.

The next day I called in sick. I could not imagine

returning to the office, returning to Paul. The morning after that, I awoke to a strange sensation in my right arm. It felt heavy. It felt numb. I couldn't lift it and it would just hang on my side. I took a shower and dressed using my left hand. I sat down at the table and ate breakfast with my left hand— my right arm resting on my lap. And there was something else I noticed: I felt smaller, as if I had suddenly shrunk. The table seemed higher. I mentioned it to James. "You're imagining things," he said.

What was wrong with me? Why did I react so strongly to such a small incident? And from such a small-minded man as Paul? I could not go back to work and face my co-workers and I especially could not face Paul. I could no longer feel comfortable at the office and with the strange paralysis of my arm, I could not be expected to do my job even if I had wanted to. I had no choice but to stay home, home where it was safe.

Still, the paralysis was worrisome and I went to see our family physician. Dr. Enright ordered x-rays and a brain scan. Everything came back negative. "There's nothing physically wrong with you, Marcelle," he said. "I'm going to refer you to another doctor. Dr. Gisvold. He's a psychiatrist. I think maybe he can help."

I couldn't get an appointment to see Dr. Gisvold for two weeks. In the interim, the arm was getting no better and soon I was becoming anxious and scared. Thinking the paralysis was psychological was particularly upsetting; I feared I was losing control of my mind. One morning I asked James to stay with me. "James, please stay with me.

I'm scared," I told him. "Please stay home. I don't want to be alone. I don't know what's happening with me." But James went to work. When he came home that evening he had the name of another psychiatrist, a name someone in his office had given him, a Dr. Boswell in San Francisco. He had already set up an appointment with Boswell for the next day. I felt relieved.

On the way to Dr. Boswell's office, I was giddy, almost childlike. Somehow, in the anticipation of opening up to this stranger, I felt oddly disconnected from myself. Walking behind James on the busy downtown San Francisco streets, I found myself humming, sometimes skipping, spelling out words on street signs, stopping in front of shop windows. James walked impatiently ahead, not looking back until he reached the door of Dr. Boswell's office building, holding it open for me, but then dashing ahead of me towards the elevator as though he didn't want anyone to know we were together.

On the twenty-seventh floor we found Dr. Boswell's office. "Hypno-Therapy, Dr. Louis Boswell," read the sign, and I spelled that out, too, embarrassing James. He took the forms from the receptionist and filled them out while I sat in a chair, swinging my feet back and forth under the seat, still humming to myself. Soon I was led into the doctor's office.

Dr. Boswell was pleasant and welcoming. Tall and thin, mid-forties, he wore a chestnut-colored suit of leather. Very San Franciscan, I thought. He had a nice smile and I felt comfortable right away. "Marcelle," he said, "your husband called saying you're having some problems. Can you tell me about them?"

"Well," I heard myself say, "I know how to spell Paul. P–A–U–L. And I know how to spell it in French, too."

"Who's Paul?" he said.

"He's my boss. But I really don't want to talk about it," I said, staring now at the floor.

"And what are you here for, Marcelle?"

"Because of Paul."

"Marcelle, do you think you can draw a picture of Paul?" He handed me a pencil and a piece of paper. I saw myself drawing a circle with eyes and then a hand reaching up to pick at a pimple.

"Do you like Paul, Marcelle?"

"Other people like him."

"But do you like him?"

"My arm hurts. I can barely move it."

Dr. Boswell nodded thoughtfully. "Marcelle," he said at last, "would you like to lie on this chair? What I would like to do is to try to get you to relax. Enough so that it will be easier for you to talk about Paul. Would that be okay?"

I moved obediently to the comfortable recliner and sat back while Dr. Boswell positioned it to where I was soon lying down. Then he covered me with a wool blanket, drawing it up under my chin. He placed a pair of headphones on me and said, "You'll hear my voice through the headphones, Marcelle. I just want you to relax and be comfortable and listen to my voice."

"Will you stay here with me?"

"I'll be right next door, Marcelle."

Soon I heard Dr. Boswell's voice in my ears. "You're feeling very relaxed," the voice said. "Your feet are heavy. Your legs are heavy. Your body is heavy. Your shoulders are relaxed. Your head is clear and you're feeling sleepy. So sleepy. Close your eyes and let yourself sleep." I went into trance easily; I had always done what I was told.

"Go back, Marcelle," the disembodied voice continued. "Go back to a time when you were very young. You are happy. You have no worries. Do you remember how old you were?" I was a little girl again, playing with a doll, giggling.

Boswell continued: "Just relax. You're still feeling very sleepy. Relax and now think back to the most frightening thing you can remember."

"No," I heard myself say immediately. "Please don't make me think of that. Please. No."

"Think back, Marcelle. What is it that is frightening you so?"

It came to me suddenly and intensely and I could not stop it. I screamed and began to punch at the air, fighting something or someone. It was terrifying. It was real. Though I had no idea what or whom I was fighting, the feeling was unrelenting and I was certain I was going to die. Boswell, alarmed, tried to bring me back. In the background, seemingly far away, I could hear his voice telling me to relax, to come back to the present. *I didn't do anything!* I heard myself cry. Eventually, I stopped screaming and fighting but when I came back to the room I was sobbing and trembling. "What happened? I asked Dr. Boswell, still terrified, my voice breaking. I left his office in shock.

I was drained and exhausted when we got home but intensely curious as to what I'd been fighting. This would be another turning point in my life. One I could not store away. This was very real. Something had happened to me and I knew I had to find out more.

I kept the appointment I'd already set up with Dr. Gisvold and went to see him before my next appointment with Boswell. Gisvold was in Petaluma, much closer than Boswell. He had a quiet demeanor, relaxed and nonchalant. He wore a drab suit and glasses. Unlike Boswell, Dr. Gisvold was more of a "talk" therapist. He listened, asking occasional questions. I talked about my life, as much of it as I could remember. He asked about my family, my childhood, my parents. "You cannot say anything bad about my father," I cautioned him. "I can say things about him, but not you." I couldn't tell if talking to him was helpful, but I knew that I needed to talk to someone. I knew I needed professional help.

I would go back to Dr. Boswell in San Francisco a couple of times. The sessions were relaxation sessions where I was to imagine walking on a beach or in the woods. He didn't try to take me back to my childhood again. Dr. Boswell suggested that he could work with Dr. Gisvold, but Dr. Gisvold would not work with him. Gisvold thought it would best for me to limit my efforts to only one therapist at a time and I decided to stay with Gisvold.

Yet I needed to know more about what Dr. Boswell had begun to uncover and my curiosity soon turned to obsession. It became more important for me than even the arm paralysis, which by then was beginning to go away on its own. What had I been fighting? What was it that was trying to kill me?

I soon came to the realization that I had very little memory of my childhood. And something else was beginning to bother me, something I needed to talk to Dr. Gisvold about. It became urgent. I could not keep it inside anymore. The hypnosis had sparked it somehow, though I wasn't sure exactly what the connection was. In the days leading up to my next appointment, it was all I could think about. And there was no one else to talk to. No one else to share the pain with.

When I went to his office, he was running late. There were other people waiting for him. I paced nervously, unable to sit down. Finally, he arrived and could only give me twenty minutes. What was inside of me had been building up and the words came spilling out hurriedly. "My brother killed my father," I told him, relating the story Louise had told me, the story that I had hidden away. It had come to the surface. And I remembered the newspaper headline. *Patricide in Mégantic.* "I read it a long time ago," I said to Dr. Gisvold, "but I could not tell anyone. Philippe was just seventeen. They were at our summer chalet. My father had gone into Lac-Mégantic that morning, to his barber shop. He'd left Philippe with instructions to pick, I think, the potatoes from the garden. Philippe didn't pick them that morning. Instead he played around. I don't know, I suppose he felt he had all day to do it. He had just turned seventeen.

My father had gone into Mégantic. Did I say that already? I am so tired. He, my father, had gone into his barber shop and Philippe had taken the rifle and was shooting out into the lake from the second-floor window of the chalet and my father came over to bring him lunch. Philippe wasn't expecting him, I'm sure. The potatoes weren't picked. He heard my father walk in and call his name. He must have known what was coming. He was terrified of my father. He panicked. He heard my father coming up the steps and Philippe had the rifle in his hand. He raised it and shot. My father fell backwards, down the steps. Philippe—he didn't want another beating."

I drove home very slowly. I needed to talk to Dr. Gisvold some more, but it would have to wait until Thursday. Three days. It seemed like forever.

CHAPTER FIVE
"est"

~

I WAS DAZED THE NIGHT I CAME HOME FROM DR. Gisvold's office after telling him what had been apparently bottled up inside of me. I knew I had done the right thing; I only wished I could have had some feedback. I felt incomplete. But there was hope. Finally, there was a chance to talk to someone about my father's death, something I hadn't talked about to anyone in eighteen years. It had been put away. There were feelings I hadn't explored in all that time, feelings I didn't even know I had. We could begin to uncover what I'd been repressing. There was now a chance that someone could help me understand what was going on with me.

And there was so much more to tell. Dr. Gisvold had been able to give me only twenty minutes that day. He had apologized for running late but there had been others waiting and we had had to make another appointment, for three days later. It was maddening. I had left his office without any kind of assessment or idea as to what the memory meant and why I had been repressing it. It was as if a wound had been opened and the doctor had told me to come back in three days to close it.

Meanwhile, something strange had begun happening on the very evening of my telling Dr. Gisvold about my father's death. It started with what I imagined to be my normal period, but before long there was an unusually heavy flow. The following day, a Tuesday, I was hemorrhaging blood. For the next couple days, I stayed mostly in bed; it was worse when I was up and walking and I was soon feeling weak and shaky. But it didn't occur to me to do anything about it.

James seemed unconcerned and though I was still hemorrhaging, when Thursday came around, he went to work as usual. That morning I asked Serge to stay home from school to drive me to Dr. Gisvold's office for the rescheduled appointment. It was imperative that I got there on time.

I walked into Dr. Gisvold's office pale and enervated. I was having trouble breathing and I had to sit down.

"Marcelle," Dr. Gisvold said. "What's going on?" I told him I was hemorrhaging. He wanted to call for an ambulance.

"No," I said. "Please. I need to talk to you. Remember, we didn't finish our talk on Monday and it's been bothering me."

"It can wait, Marcelle. We need to get you to the hospital."

I was disappointed. "Serge can take me," I told him.

Dr. Gisvold called Serge into his interior office and told him to drive directly to the emergency entrance. Then he called ahead to the hospital and emergency room personnel were waiting when we arrived.

At the hospital they immediately began an I.V. and hooked me to an EKG machine and ran numerous tests and then started blood transfusions. After receiving blood, I was still hemorrhaging and they decided on surgery: a D&C— dilation and curettage –, a procedure to stop the bleeding. The surgery lasted an hour and a half. When I awoke I was still receiving blood. In all, they would replace five pints.

Danny and Alain came into the intensive care to visit while I was recovering. They had walked almost three miles to come see me. I was still on the EKG machine and there were various tubes connected to me and I had a mask over my mouth and nose and Alain began to cry. Later, a nurse told me that another few hours of hemorrhaging and I might have died. Lying in my hospital bed this was strange for me to hear because for some reason it didn't seem as though it was really me who had been bleeding. It didn't occur to me that it was *my* life that had been in danger. At the same time, the hemorrhaging had seemed oddly cleansing to me, especially coming on the heels of my cathartic session with Dr. Gisvold. It felt almost necessary somehow.

Later I would wonder at the experience. Why had I not sought help earlier? Why had I remained passively in bed while I had been essentially bleeding to death? I couldn't help but wonder if I was subconsciously trying to do away with myself. Or—maybe—a part of myself. It was frightening and I started to think that maybe I was beginning to lose my sanity.

I mentioned it to James. We were sitting at the kitchen table the day I came home from the hospital and I told him how strange it was to think that I did not ask for help. I wondered if it could have been an unconscious attempt at suicide. "Maybe," James said. "If you want to kill yourself there's an easier way, you know. Park the car in the garage and leave the engine running. You won't feel any pain at all. You'll just go to sleep and never wake up." I stared back at him, speechless. I had been trying not to judge him for doing nothing while I had been bleeding to death. Why had not he done anything to help me? Was he hoping to find me dead when he came home from work?

When I returned to see Dr. Gisvold a few days after I was released from the hospital, we talked about what James had said and he expressed surprise at his insensitivity. We talked more about my father but he soon had me talking about my mother, too. "Maybe there's something with your mother that you've repressed," he suggested. I knew that was not it, but I didn't know how to tell him. Truthfully, I didn't know what to say to Dr. Gisvold and for his part, he didn't seem to know how to get out of me what he needed. I told him I feared I was having a breakdown but he dismissed the idea. "You're not having a breakdown," he said, almost impatiently. "A breakdown would be much different."

I continued to see Dr. Gisvold for almost a year, even

though my arm paralysis had been completely resolved after about a month. Gradually I'd been able to start using my arm more and more. Gisvold's explanation was that the paralysis was a mechanism initiated by my subconscious mind to prevent me from acting impulsively and striking Paul, the apparent object of my purported anger and the underlying reason for my troubles. I knew it ran deeper and I became consumed with finding out more about the assault I had experienced under hypnosis.

But the sessions with Dr. Gisvold continued to consist mostly of me talking and him listening, asking questions here and there. He was frequently late and I often felt rushed. I wanted to speak more about the incident in Dr. Boswell's office, but Gisvold was uninterested in pursuing it. Sometimes I felt as though he wasn't really listening. He'd look at me as I'd speak but for all I knew he was thinking about his next appointment or planning his evening. Eventually I felt I was getting nothing out of the sessions at all. For the most part, we were just killing time.

But I had visions every now and then, very quick glimpses of things—a basement with a dirt floor, a furnace, cords of wood. And an urgent sense of wanting to flee, of wanting to hide. What did it all mean?

I had a good friend, Madeleine, my first real friend in Petaluma. She and I had become like sisters. We bicycled together, went out to breakfast, went shopping. We walked together and talked a lot. I got to know her husband Hiro, too. The two had timeshares in Tahoe and Mexico and they often invited James and me along, or would ask if we wanted to buy into the timeshares. They invested in various products, too, the latest innovations, and they would try to include us in the investment opportunities. They were up on the current trends and they joined all sorts of groups, continually trying new and different things.

Madeleine knew something of my childhood turmoil, at least what little of it I could relate to her. She knew all about my trips to Gisvold's office and my frustration. She had confided to me about her own childhood as well, and I suppose it was only natural that she would tell me about a new group she and Hiro had joined. "It's called 'est'," she said. "It's a kind of self-help training. It's in a group setting and it's like this really, really intense seminar that takes place over the course of a couple of weekends. It's all about self-awareness. It's…well, it's hard for me to describe. But you learn a lot about yourself, Marcelle. I think it could help you."

Madeleine gave me a brochure. "The purpose of the *est* training," it read, quoting the training's founder, Werner Erhard (est actually stood for Erhard Seminars Training), "is to transform your ability to experience living so that the situations you have been trying to change or have been putting up with clear up just in the process of life itself."

I was intrigued but skeptical. For one thing, I didn't much care for group settings. But I asked Dr. Gisvold about est and he seemed rather informed about it. "It might help, Marcelle," he said. "It might be good for you. Yes, I would advise you to do it."

There was a pre-training seminar on the Monday

leading up to the first weekend of training. There, we were given a rough idea of what to expect. The first day's training, Saturday, would start at 8:30 a.m. and would last until 11:00 p.m. or even later. It could be fifteen straight hours or more. Watches were not allowed. There would be, perhaps, two breaks all day. A lunch break wouldn't occur until late in the afternoon. The second day would start at 9:00 a.m. and run just as late. A mid-training seminar would be held the following Tuesday evening and then the next weekend would be another grueling two days. "We're going to tear you down and put you back together," we were told.

I continued to be apprehensive and the pre-training seminar did little to alleviate my apprehension. But I'd become desperate. I wanted to know what was wrong with me. Gisvold seemed unwilling, or perhaps unable, to deal with me, with the memories of my childhood that were, by then, so obviously repressed. I needed to try something. Anything. I deferred to Gisvold's advice and to Madeleine's recommendation. I made up my mind to go, believing I had nothing to lose.

Saturday's session was at the Hotel Leamington in Oakland. There were probably two hundred of us, seated in rows of straight-backed chairs in a large conference hall. The trainer, Ron, took the stage and barked into the microphone. "No talking." The room became quiet. He continued: "You are here because your lives do not work. You are hopeless. You don't know what you're doing. You don't know how to experience life. You are struggling. You are desperate and confused. In brief, your lives are shit." It seemed an odd introduction, but his words somehow resonated with me. Ron was firm, but there was pleasant nature about him. He was small and probably no more than thirty but he had a certain charisma and I felt his confidence. Maybe, I thought, I've found the place where I can learn what's going on with me.

Then Ron went on to describe the stress and discomfort and anxiety we were going to feel in the long hours ahead. He was smiling, taking pleasure in the words. We would inevitably crack, he assured us, after hours and hours of being deprived of talking, of standing up, of leaving the room, of smoking, of going to the bathroom. We would feel boredom, anger, frustration, and ripped off, until, he told us, "you finally begin to get that you'll do anything to keep from experiencing what is actually happening to you." And then he reiterated the objective outlined for us at the pre-training seminar: "We're going to tear you down and put you back together."

Over the course of that day, and the next one (held in a similar room at the Fairmount Hotel in San Francisco), and the following weekend (Holiday Inn Golden Gateway on Saturday and Jack Tar Hotel on Sunday)—a total of over 50 hours—I came to regard est for what it really was: an insidious form of brainwashing. It was mass hypnosis. At first I was reminded of a time when I was fifteen and "The Great Robert" came to town, a hypnotist who entertained the crowd by making volunteers do funny things to his commands. But very quickly I could see that this was not entertainment.

Throughout the long days, Ron, and sometimes other trainers, would saunter around the room, talking hypnotically, or else berating us, while we all sat, eyes closed, listening while our minds started to melt away. We were told that our belief systems were useless. Reason, logic, and understanding were "non-experiential"; they were second-hand mental exercises that needed to be abandoned if we were to advance in life. We were told that our problems were never caused by others or by circumstance; they were always self-inflicted. We were told to concentrate on our pain. We were told our minds were like machines and nothing more, but if we accepted the nature of our minds, healing could begin. We could accept that we are what we have always wanted to be. It was all very existential, but delivered in an almost mystical way by Ron and the other trainers who spoke as gurus, with secrets that would be unveiled to us as the days of training would proceed. There was an epiphany awaiting each of us.

Through the long days, the hypnotic effect of the training led to hallucinatory images for me. There were strong religious implications to what I was seeing and at one point, I was in a church. I didn't recognize it but it had rich, beautiful wood, and for some reason it seemed like such a sad place to be. At one particular point, very early on in the training, I heard myself say in a low voice, *he killed him*, and I knew I was referring to Philippe and my father.

Towards the beginning of the training we were directed to create an imagined "space" around us, a circle that was to be ours and ours alone. No one could enter the space. We carried this space with us throughout the duration of the training. At the end of the training, Ron told us to allow someone into our space. The person would be a surprise to us. "Someone from the past, perhaps," he said. "Someone with whom you have unresolved issues maybe. Make peace with them. Let them in. Just let it happen and accept whoever walks into your space."

It was a nun.

Oh, no, I heard myself say. I couldn't see the nun's face, only her dark habit. I had no idea what she represented but her sudden presence was overwhelming and I began to shiver and I fell down to my knees and I was soon sobbing uncontrollably. I started to hyperventilate and felt as though I might pass out. At that moment, I heard Ron telling us to say goodbye to the person in our space, and the nun was gone. I began to breathe again.

Tears were still running down my face when Ron finally closed out the training. The vast majority of the attendees seemed strangely ecstatic to me. Through the course of the training, they had "gotten it." For me, I was left undone and I knew with a sense of despair that there could be no shortcut. Not for me. My life would still not work. My situation would not clear up "just in the process of life itself." I felt hopelessly lost.

Ron congratulated the room but before excusing us he looked straight at me and said, "Ah, but I see some of you in here are still little girls." Then he walked over to me and smiled and embraced me, lifting me off my feet. It was an exceedingly odd moment and through my exhausted confusion I wondered if Ron knew that the est training had only produced half its advertised effect. It had only torn me down.

CHAPTER SIX

Ross Valley

~

FOR HER PART, MADELEINE FELT TERRIBLE ABOUT MY est experience. "I'm so sorry," she kept saying. "Hiro and I are both really sorry. It was such a great experience for us. Look, Marcelle, if there's anything you need, just let us know. Day or night. We're here for you."

As for Gisvold, I could not return to him. His recommending est was the final straw. Madeleine was a friend trying to help. Gisvold was a trained psychiatrist. I had initially gone to him with a psychosomatic paralysis. I had unloaded hidden memories of my father's death. I had gone into shock and had almost bled to death. Then for a year all we did was talk, at the end of which time he could do nothing but recommend a dubious, trendy therapy. Clearly there was something hidden in my past, something buried deep within. There were enough clues for a competent psychiatrist to do something meaningful with them.

Gisvold had done nothing.

It was shortly after the est training that I had the experience in the kitchen where I made the discovery that the seven-year-old girl in my vision was me. And before long, it felt as though she was becoming alive inside of me; it was as though she was taking over. I was scared of being alone. I lay awake at nights, afraid to fall asleep, afraid of waking up as someone else.

Then one day, there was another incident in the kitchen. I was home alone and my eyes came to rest on something on the kitchen counter. I don't remember what it was. A plate? A napkin holder? Whatever it was, it suddenly became a dagger. And in that instant I felt the presence of someone—a girl, perhaps twelve years old. She was wearing a school uniform and she was wielding the dagger and she was striking downward with it repeatedly, violently. It wasn't anything I could see; it was, rather, a distinct and unmistakable impression, a sudden awareness. A vicious and palpable anger emanated from the girl and I became terrified. I ran out of the house into the backyard and walked around for quite some time, until I felt in control again. When I finally went back inside, the kitchen was as it always was.

Over the course of the next few days I tried to make sense of what I'd felt in the kitchen. Was it my own pent-up rage, my frustration over my situation—making no progress with Gisvold, being ripped apart by the est training? Why the school uniform? Why a twelve-year-old girl? I thought of the seven-year-old girl in the vision I had always carried with me. What was the connection? Years later I would wonder if I had been getting too close to that seven-year-old. I would wonder if the twelve-year-old was brought about somehow as a protector.

I didn't tell anyone about the knife episode but I asked my oldest son Jacques to help me find another psychiatrist. Jacques was twenty-two by then, just home from the service. He was concerned. He knew something was wrong with me. He tried to understand and for that I was grateful, but I could not adequately explain to him what it was. "Sometimes I remember things," I told him. "And then other times I can't, and it feels as though I somehow change personalities."

"Then we'll get you some help, Mom," he said. "We'll find someone you can talk to."

James, meanwhile, was busy with work and took very little notice of what was happening to me. Maybe he was thinking that if he just ignored it, it would somehow resolve itself. Most likely he felt helpless; he didn't understand what was going on (I didn't understand it myself, after all) and he had no idea what to do with me. I had become a burden to him.

Jacques found a psychiatrist in Marin County, Dr. James Mickle, and came along with me to my first appointment. Dr. Mickle was in an office suite that was shared by several practitioners, one of whom turned out to be Dr. Gisvold. I knew Gisvold had an office in Marin County—indeed it's why he had so often been late for his appointments in Petaluma—but of course I had no idea where. It turned out the two doctors knew each other. Sometimes they would fill in for each other. I wondered if they compared notes.

Dr Mickle was tall and wore a smart, navy-colored suit that set off his blue eyes. He introduced himself and asked some questions and I began to open up to him, but I don't imagine I made a lot of sense. There was much I wanted to say. I would start a sentence and then break it off, thinking of something else. The days and weeks after est were tremendously bewildering for me and I hardly knew how to communicate what I felt. It was as though the est training had too quickly opened doors that I was not ready to peer into.

I wondered, as I had with Gisvold, if Dr. Mickle believed me. I didn't mention the twelve-year-old girl, nor the seven-year-old girl. I had read *The Three Faces of Eve* some years prior, a book based on a case study of multiple personality disorder and the book struck me as sensationalistic and exaggerated, maybe even phony. I didn't want to appear to Dr. Mickle as histrionic. I needed him to believe me, to understand me. I ended up talking to him about my absence of solid memories from my early childhood. But I did confide that I was becoming more and more confused as to who I really was.

We set up another appointment but my life was becoming chaotic. Adding to my own personal turmoil was that I had discovered Alain and Danny were becoming involved with drugs. One day I found two bags of what I suspected was marijuana in Alain's bedroom. When I confronted him he told me it belonged to the school custodian. I felt powerless and afraid—powerless to help my sons, and afraid of them, too. Alcohol and drugs had always frightened me, back to my days with Aldéma. And even before then. I didn't want to call the police because I didn't want to get my kids into trouble. In hindsight, I probably should have. In time, I would see both Alain and Danny change from sweet kids to young men addicted to alcohol and drugs.

I hid the two bags of marijuana, undecided what to do with it. A few days later, Alain came to me and told me the custodian was after him for the money. I told him to have the custodian come and pick up the bags. The custodian was a tall, slim, blond-haired young man. In addition to working for the school, he raised sheep that he kept on a rented piece of property on the outskirts of town. He came by and I told him to consider himself lucky that I didn't have the police there to pick him up. And I told him to stay away from my kids.

Meanwhile, I was gaining a sense that my emotional problems had been brought about by myself. I had refused to deal with something in my past. That something was now creeping into my life, breaching whatever barriers I had erected along the way. It was time to pay for all the hiding and I sensed the cost was going to be steep. Barbra Streisand had just released "The Way We Were," and it would play on the radio and I would listen and wonder why I couldn't go back, back before the seven-year-old girl, back to the way we were. But of course I knew it was impossible. One can never go back.

And I couldn't get the vision of the girl with the dagger

out of my mind. It stood to reason that if the seven-year-old was inside of me, the twelve-year-old must have been, too. What if I woke up as her? She was especially disturbing as I had always been a passive person, often fearful. Never violent. My sense was that a loss of control for me would be no less than life threatening.

One day I came across a photograph of myself. It had been taken in our backyard at our house on Champlain Street. I was wearing a school uniform and a long white veil covered my head and ran down the length of the uniform. Most likely, the photo had been taken on the day I made my *Communion Solennelle*. Catholic custom was that children make their first Communion around seven and "Solemn Communion" at twelve or thirteen. Perhaps the catechism I had been studying in the living room that day when my nose began to bleed was for this very Communion. It might well have been my last catechism exam. That's why it was so important. If I did not pass it, I could not have been confirmed.

I looked ugly in the picture. I took a lighter and burned the picture and watched it smolder in the ashtray. At the time, it seemed important to do so. It seemed important to try to rid myself of something—of some part of me. It was a cleansing attempt, as the hemorrhaging may have been, only it was more consciously undertaken. I treated it like a ritual, an essential act on the road toward healing. I felt a slight change come over me afterwards. I felt a little stronger. I didn't reach the angry twelve-year-old that day, but somehow I felt I had accomplished something. I had started fighting back, and even though I could not have said exactly what or whom I was fighting, I knew a war of sorts had begun.

But the seven-year-old continued to get stronger. I felt she was the one who seemed most immediately threatening, the one most likely to take control of me. I knew I needed close supervision. It was still a few days before my next appointment with Dr. Mickle but I drove to his office and told him I needed to be hospitalized.

"What's going on?" he asked.

"I'm confused. I can't sleep. I feel as if I'm losing my mind and I don't feel safe. I need a safe place. I need protection. I need to know what's happening to me. I want to feel safe."

Dr. Mickle prescribed some medication and then arranged for me to be admitted to the Ross Valley Psychiatric Hospital. I drove there myself and checked in. Ross Valley was an imposing three-story, red brick building. The rooms on the second floor were for people with mental illnesses; the third floor was for drug and alcohol patients. Upon admittance, they escorted me to my room, next to the nurse's station on the second floor, and I immediately walked over to the window. I needed to know it was secure, that it couldn't be opened. If the little girl took over while I slept, might she try to make for the window? Might she jump?

I spent eight days at Ross Valley. Dr. Mickle came once a day. On the second day I decided to confess to him my real fear—that a little girl inside me might take over. I knew I needed to tell him but the prospect made me nervous, even panicky. I needed his understanding and the little girl was embarrassing to me. What if he didn't understand? What if he did not believe me? I tried to calm myself as best I could and told myself I was in the right place and Dr. Mickle was the right person to confide in. And so I told him.

"She's seven in the vision," I began. "She's on a bed and she's lifeless and there are prayer candles on her chest. There is a nun in the room. I know now that the little girl was me. I must have thought I was dead because I have a clear vision in my mind of seeing myself from the ceiling, of floating there. I remember little else. And as I have told you, I remember practically nothing from my childhood. But now I know the little girl is alive. And I sense very strongly that she wants to take over. Please, Dr. Mickle. Please don't let that happen. Please don't let the little girl take over."

Dr. Mickle listened patiently and then said, very calmly, "Marcelle, let's examine this logically. Okay? Now, where are you?"

"Ross Valley."

"And who is here? In this room?"

"You and I."

"And do you see anyone else?"

"No."

"Do you see a seven-year-old girl in here?"

"No."

"Of course not. Now, try to relax. The medication will help you and the staff here is top-notch. I'll be back tomorrow to check on you." Dr. Mickle walked out of my room and I felt embarrassed. He was right of course. There was no little girl in the room. Even I hadn't seen her outside of the vision in my head. Dr. Mickle was going to be no help to me and neither was the hospital. I should have checked out right then. My admittance was voluntary, after all, and I could leave anytime I wanted. But I was still scared and still in need of a secure place. I stayed.

For the next several days I did what the staff said. There were group therapy sessions with other patients. There was an afternoon trip to Golden Gate Park. There were arts and crafts and we made pottery. One morning they took us to a little greenhouse area of the hospital. I don't remember exactly why; to spend time tending plants, perhaps. Covered, and with a dirt floor, the area was dimly lit and reminded me of a basement. One of the patients had a small hand shovel and he was hitting at the ground with it, digging up dirt. For some reason, the digging threw me into a panic. Trembling, I turned and ran upstairs to my room.

They continued to medicate me and over time I came to feel empty inside, like I was some sort of zombie. When I first checked into the hospital I saw medicated patients from the ward walking around with blank looks on their faces. I overheard someone say that most of these patients were repeaters—they'd go home and then come back, time and time again. Now I began to realize that I was one of the people walking blankly around. Was I destined to become a repeater, too? Was this my future?

I awoke one morning and decided I needed fresh air. I asked for a pass and through my medicated haze I walked down the street to a small café not far from the hospital. I ordered coffee and sat at a table. I considered that although the hospital provided for me some security, it was coming at too high a price. The hospital could not, it seemed to me, provide me with what I really needed. The medication was calming me down, but it was only treating the symptoms. It was a band-aid over the open wound. By then, Dr. Mickle was actively discouraging me from talking about my past. I sensed he thought that my references to my past, and to the little girl especially, were melodramatic, even disingenuous. No one seemed interested in getting to the root of my despondency.

I wondered if I should check out. While I sat there considering my options my eyes came to rest on a bulletin board on the wall of the café. Amid the posted notices and announcements, someone had thumb tacked a small flyer with these words:

We, the unwilling,
Led by the unqualified,
Have done so much for so long,
We are now doing the impossible,
With nothing at all.

I jotted the passage down and when I returned to the hospital, I taped it to the headboard of my bed. The next morning, I checked myself out.

CHAPTER SEVEN
Brookwood

∿

AFTER ROSS VALLEY IT STARTED TO BECOME MORE important to me to try to remember what I had been repressing. But I also sensed that I was not ready to recollect all of it at once. I prayed to have it revealed to me gradually. I was in the bedroom one day and it occurred to me that if I just lay down on the bed, maybe the memories would come to me slowly in a dream. I asked God to help me remember. Surely He could see how miserable I was. Before closing my eyes, I tried to clear my mind and I prayed for a miracle. When I opened my eyes again I found myself puzzled by what I had just seen. I'd had a clear vision of some sort of tragic event and, just as I had asked, the vision had come in slowly. But it had come in as something of a mystery to be solved. As though a curtain was being slowly lifted, the vision revealed first one young boy, and then another. Both were blonde and lying on the floor. Both were being beaten fiercely. It was as if the vision was of two different scenes and the scenes were alternating. But the curtain wouldn't lift high enough to where I could see who was beating the young boys.

I couldn't stop thinking about the vision and it was too real to dismiss. The next day I called one of my sisters and told her what I had seen.

"Philippe and Gaston," she said. "Don't you remember, Marcelle?"

"No. What about Philippe and Gaston?"

"You don't remember Father beating them both so badly?"

I had not remembered. I didn't recall the beatings still. But the confirmation from my sister as to what I had envisioned led me to believe that I had memories of those scenes somewhere in my mind and that the memories were not false ones. And I wondered what else my mind was harboring, what else it had been keeping from me.

I saw Dr. Mickle once more after Ross Valley. I held out some hope that he could help me but I made it clear to him that I wanted nothing more to do with the medication he'd been prescribing. My request did not go over well.

"Well, Marcelle," he said, rising and offering me his hand to shake, "it doesn't seem as if you need me anymore then. You're always welcome to call upon me, of course, if you find yourself in a desperate situation and there is no one else, but it looks as though I can be of no further help to you at this time." It was shocking to hear and I wondered if I should relent and take the drugs. Then I thought of the people walking like zombies at the hospital and I determined that I was no going to become like them.

I went home feeling abandoned and alone. I wondered if Dr. Mickle had seen the poster that I had taped to my headboard before leaving Ross Valley and if the poster was the reason for his dismissal of me. Part of me regretted the poster. But why hadn't he said anything? Dr. Mickle was a psychiatrist, supposedly a good communicator. In time I would come to feel as though Dr. Mickle had no real understanding of what I was going through. Most likely, he believed I could not make it without prescribed drugs; I would return to Ross Valley and beg for them.

Meanwhile, I had filed for worker's compensation. I hadn't been able to work in over a year and the assistant manager at Host had told me to file. I saw a worker's comp attorney who referred me for a diagnosis to a forensic psychiatrist in Mill Valley by the name of Dr. Martin Blinder. Blinder would become somewhat famous just two years later as a witness for the defense of the man who would assassinate San Francisco mayor George Moscone and city supervisor Harvey Milk. The defense would argue that the killer had been depressed, with mood swings that had been exacerbated by his consumption of junk food. The strategy became known pejoratively as the Twinkie defense.

Dr. Blinder interviewed me in his Mill Valley office, asking a variety of what seemed like standard questions, mostly related to work. Then one caught me off guard. "How's your sex life?" he asked.

"Can we not speak about that?" I said and I started to

cry, almost hysterically. The crying surprised me. I had come in well prepared. I had not wanted to appear emotional.

"Of course," Dr. Blinder said. "But I think this is something that should be explored." He asked a few more questions and the interview was over. Then he asked me if I was seeing a psychiatrist or therapist. I told him about Dr. Mickle's dismissal and that I had not seen anyone else since. "I'm going to recommend someone I think can help you," he said. "His name is Jim Fraser. He's an MFCC—marriage, family, and child counselor. He has an office not far from you in Santa Rosa."

I began to see Jim Fraser on a weekly basis and I liked him. I judged him to be a few years younger than I. He was tall with reddish blonde hair and clear blue eyes. He was relaxed in his manner of speaking and he made me feel comfortable immediately. He was sensitive and warm and easy to talk to. He asked a lot of questions, digging into my life very effectively and quickly ascertaining that my marriage wasn't working. In time, we would have a few sessions with James and the boys.

The problem, though, was that Jim had very little experience with repressed memories. He helped with the surface issues that were going on in my life at the time, but he had difficulty digging deeper. He was a counselor, after all, and not a psychiatrist. When I spoke about my childhood and my loss of memories, we made little headway. I didn't want to talk about the little girl in me—afraid he would not believe me and I'd end up abandoned again. We talked about my relationship with James and with that he was helpful.

Jim cared and he tried harder than the others, but I was still feeling out of control. The seven-year-old girl was not going away and I still had no idea what she represented.

During one session, I told Jim about my lifelong fear of being alone at night, of having my door smashed open and of being physically attacked. "How about if we try some self-defense techniques, Marcelle?" he suggested. "These might help you feel more empowered. Make you feel stronger and more confident. Want to try?"

"Sure," I said.

"Here, lie down on the floor. Now, fight back as hard as you can and don't worry about hurting me."

But when Jim bent down and moved towards me, I suddenly panicked, going into a sort of frenzy. I screamed and rolled away from him and dodged around the office, looking for a place to hide and then ran towards a window, seeking a way out, finally scurrying into a corner, crouched down, back against the wall, seething and scared, like a wild animal.

Eventually, after quite a while, Jim was able to calm me down.

For several days after that episode, I lived in fear. I slept very little. If I had felt out of control before, I felt much more so now. I was rapidly losing my grip on my sanity and one morning in particular I felt myself breaking apart and it was then that I drove to Jim's office, Petula Clark singing "Downtown" on the car radio. Once again I needed a safe environment. I needed security. I had told Dr. Mickle and he had not believed me. Maybe Jim Fraser would. "There is a little girl in me," I said when I arrived at his office, "and she wants to take over." Jim had other appointments but he let me wait for him upstairs. Several hours later, late in the afternoon, he accompanied me to Brookwood Hospital and I was checked in.

Later that evening, after dinner, there was group therapy and I met Dr. Chamberlin, the hospital psychiatrist. Somewhere during the session I apparently confessed my distrust of the psychiatric profession and its level of competency, though I have only a partial recollection of what I said: "I will write a book someday and I'll tell others all about it." From that moment on, I felt a shift in the attitude from the staff. They were distant and seemed suspicious and I sensed that I was not welcomed there. At one point I overheard one nurse tell another, "I think this one's only here to inspect the facility."

Jim Fraser came in every day for one-on-one therapy, something the staff at Brookwood seemed to resent. Jim was not a licensed psychiatrist and I imagine his counseling sessions with me were probably considered superfluous, maybe even unwise. Brookwood had trained, expert psychiatrists on duty, after all. But I trusted Jim and I wanted to see him every day.

At the same group meeting where I apparently slighted the psychiatric profession, I said something else. Every day since, for thirty-seven years, I have tried to find out what. I would even ask Jim Fraser to contact Brookwood on my behalf to find out, but the staff refused to disclose any information about me. I know only that I spoke of a terrible tragedy, one I sensed had not yet happened. A prediction of some description. Whatever it was I said, it was met with a stunned silence. And then the next thing I remember, I was saying, almost deliriously, "Oh, boy, am I rich!"

"Marcelle," said Dr. Chamberlin after my declaration, "let's go in my office for a minute." Chamberlin walked me out of the room and down the corridor and into a small office. "How do you do that?" he asked. He was standing, leaning against the wall with one foot crossed in front of the other and I noticed a hole in his shoe.

I didn't know what he was referring to but I answered him anyway. "If numbers can borrow from each other," I heard myself say, "then so can people."

"What do you mean, Marcelle?"

"Here," I said, taking a piece of paper and a pencil from a desk. "I'll show you." And I began to jot down a math problem. "Let's say you're subtracting 23 from 122. See? When I go to subtract the three from the two, I have to borrow a one from this column here. Do you see? It's like that. You meet people and you talk to them and you borrow from them. You can borrow from their minds." It seemed strange even then, even as I was saying it. I had no idea what I was talking about. Chamberlin looked at me blankly and then turned and walked out of the room.

I stayed for four days at Brookwood and then I checked myself out. I felt as though I didn't belong. Nobody understood me and it seemed as if no one was interested in finding out what my problems were. Later I would learn that Chamberlin overcharged my insurance company. And six months after my stay at Brookwood, I read in the paper where he had been arrested for having sex with an underage patient. Subsequent news accounts reported that he lost his California license to practice and was sentenced to five years in prison.

On the way home from Brookwood I found myself driving behind a box truck with the rear doors open. It was near dusk and I could just make out that the back of the truck was empty. Just a dark, empty box. And it occurred to me that if I didn't find a way to help myself, to pull myself together, to take matters into my own hands, I was going to soon find myself locked up in a box like that. A cell somewhere, in a mental hospital. Drugged, most likely. And all alone.

CHAPTER EIGHT

Working

∼

IN OCTOBER OF 1977, A MONTH AFTER I CHECKED OUT of Brookwood, I went back to work. I needed to. I needed to get back out into the world and I needed to keep my mind busy. I applied and was hired as a cashier at a nearby J.C. Penney. Chuck Lewis was the store manager and when I began to work I heard other employees talking about Mr. Lewis. They warned me about him. "He hides, and watches to make sure everybody is doing their jobs." I never witnessed that and as time went along, I found Mr. Lewis to be nothing but fair. He was a good, dedicated, honest manager. I liked him. Though I'd been hired part-time for the Christmas season, I stayed on afterwards. I felt fortunate to be working.

I continued to see Jim Fraser until the spring of 1978. By then, I was feeling better, my mind and my time having been occupied by work. But even still, the thought of the little girl was never far from my mind. Jim held a Christmas party for his patients in '77 and I had brought him a house-plant as a gift. Underneath the leaves, behind one of the stems, I had hidden a small plastic doll—a little girl. I was hoping he would discover my hint and help me find her, help me find the little girl. I just wanted someone to listen to me, to try to help me untangle the mess I was in, to help me figure out who I was. The thoughts would never leave me. Everything I did I was doing for the little girl. I wanted to touch her. I wanted to tame her so that she wouldn't be afraid anymore. I needed help, but I didn't know how to express it. I could only drop hints. Jim never noticed the little plastic doll.

I liked my job at J.C. Penney. Learning new things was always exciting for me. Once I would learn one position, I'd begin to look around for something new to learn. I became easily bored when I knew my job too well and so when I learned of an opening in the credit department at the store, I asked Mr. Lewis for the position. He consulted with the credit supervisor and I was transferred. The credit super-visor was a woman named Jane Thomas and we worked well together. In a few weeks I became her assistant. She didn't say so at the time but there was illness in her family and she was also facing a divorce. I think she anticipated taking time off in the future. Soon after my transfer to the credit depart-ment, the J.C. Penney catalog came out and it was decided that catalog sales would come under the purview of the credit department. It meant more responsibility, which I welcomed. Eventually, Jane left. I was sorry to see her leave but I understood. I felt the turmoil in her life.

I was promoted to replace Jane and I became supervisor of the credit and catalog department. I felt the promotion might have been a bit premature; I wasn't sure I could handle the job. I went home with binders and all kinds of material to read and study. I even studied in my dreams and I asked Mr. Lewis jokingly if I got paid for studying while I slept. Mr. Lewis was very helpful to me at the time, working with me so that I could make the transition, teaching me how to budget the department. I also went for a few days of training on catalog advertising and promotion. I became responsible for every angle of the catalog sales.

I typically had six or seven people in my department and upwards of a dozen during the holidays. The Christmas season was hectic. In addition to catalog sales, my department also handled the store switchboard, customer complaints, the taking of payments on J.C. Penney card accounts, and the opening of new accounts for customers. We were even responsible for gift wrap. But I had an excellent staff and my assistant, Ione, was sharp and great to work with. I felt fortunate to have such reliable people working for me. The department became very successful. There were thirty-five stores in our district and my department was always somewhere near the top in sales gains.

A good part of the success I attributed to my desire to want to make everyone feel at ease. Whenever I would interview someone for a position, I would end the interview asking them where they would feel most comfortable working—the switchboard, the front desk, gift wrap, as a typist? I would ask them what hours would best accommodate them. I ended up with a very happy staff and those were fine years for me. I was proud and I was good at my job. Years later, I would run into Jean, a former employee, a gentle woman who always wore a smile and treated customers with the utmost respect, and she would remind me of the good days at the store. "Marcelle was the best boss I ever had," she would tell anyone who asked. The work was satisfying, and therapeutic.

I kept busy at home as well. Back when we'd first moved to Petaluma, I had taken an evening class on basic automobile repair. In fact, the class is where I had met Madeleine. Her husband Hiro was in the class and Madeleine had always accompanied him. I had taken the class because I was sure there had been times I'd been taken advantage of when taking my car in for repair. James wouldn't get a driver's license until years into our marriage and so it was left to me to take the car in for service and maintenance. I dreaded doing so because I never knew exactly what the mechanics were telling me or whether I could trust them. A smallish woman mechanically disinclined and with a slight accent didn't stand a chance against the underhanded selling techniques of the male-dominated car repair industry. I decided I wanted to know what was really wrong with my car whenever the man at the shop produced a diagnosis with a questionable cost estimate. I took the class and I learned enough to do routine maintenance and small repairs myself. I enjoyed it. It felt empowering. And so when I wasn't working at the store, I was often tinkering with the car, doing tune-ups or changing the oil.

But eventually I would come to notice that while I might be doing work on the car after work, James would be in the living room reading the paper and the boys would be watching television—all of them waiting for me to come in and make dinner. I'd come into the house, my hands dirty with grease and oil, and I'd wash and start dinner for everyone as they waited. I found myself starting to resent it. Though I felt proud to be able to do the work myself, I also knew that I had put myself in a position to where I was feeling exploited. I couldn't express this to James. I felt he should have helped, but his attitude was that I owed it to him to do the work. The boys, on the other hand—I simply felt bad that I couldn't spend more time with them, that I had to go to work and not be home when they came home from school. I felt bad for many things about the boys. I knew they had a hard time with their mother being in a mixed marriage and I always tried to make up to them for the harassment I knew they got in school.

One day I began to do some maintenance on the car and found that I could do it no longer. I looked down at my dirty and greasy hands and I felt sick. I felt exhausted. The mechanic in me left that day and it felt good.

But there was other work. I worked on the house, too. James took care of the yard, but I was always fixing something up. James didn't like change. It bothered him if I so much as moved furniture around. Wallpaper or new paint or new curtains were always met with disapproval. By then I was no longer looking for any sign of appreciation from

James, but I had become concerned about the maintenance of the house. Necessary repairs weren't being done and I soon learned to do whatever I wanted and whatever was needed and simply put up with the disapprovals. I was not afraid of James. He hardly ever raised his voice at anyone and was not a violent man, for which I was grateful. His disapproval was registered typically as silence and I decided I could live with that.

The previous owner had completed several projects around the house and it was clear he was not very handy. One of the projects was a ten-foot-long bar in the family room. James didn't drink and I didn't drink and we rarely entertained. The bar was an eyesore and it always seemed in the way. I hated looking at it every time I walked by it. I wanted to take it down and I asked for James's help but he would have none of it. One day, tired of looking at the bar, I took a crowbar and dismantled it. I carried the pieces to the garage and stacked them all neatly in a corner. Then I nervously waited for James to get home. "What did you do with the bar?" he demanded when he saw the empty space. I told him and he stalked out to the garage where he looked at the stack of pieces and I became afraid that he was planning on putting the bar back together. But I never heard of it again. James was silent for a few days and life went on.

The previous owner had also blocked access to the kitchen from the dining room. He had built a wall to cover the door. I took that down, too. James shook his head when he came home. I smiled, taking it as a compliment.

The largest project the previous owner had undertaken

was a small patio deck built onto the back of the house. If the bar was an eyesore, at least only family would see it. But the patio deck, an even bigger eyesore, could be seen by all the neighbors. I wanted to take it down and have a new one built and in 1981, I talked to James about it. He refused to consider the idea. I had gone ahead and procured two contractors' estimates but true to form, James had no interest in any alterations to the status quo and he rejected both of them. I knew that on my salary alone, I couldn't afford to hire a contractor.

Over time, I began to think maybe I could do the job myself. I bought books and studied. I looked at the flimsy deck and took measurements. I came to believe I could dismantle the deck and use the redwood to rebuild it. The existing deck was about four feet off the ground, with steps that were wobbly and unsafe. I decided to make it six inches off the ground. I figured I could use the wood to make a lower deck and then hire someone to build the awnings.

I needed tools. Drills, power saws, an impact wrench. The impact wrench, one of the books said, was needed to drill through the house base to secure the ledger board to the house. I decided I could save some money by renting the drill, since I figured I'd probably never use it again. I went to the local hardware store where the young man at the customer service desk asked what I needed an impact wrench for. "I'm building a deck," I told him. "I need to drill through concrete."

He looked at me—all 5-foot, 2-inches and 105 pounds of me—and winked and smiled at the customer standing in line behind me. "How many pounds per square foot will your deck hold?" he asked. I felt embarrassed. I had no idea. What am I doing here? I thought. What made me think I could build a deck all by myself? But then anger replaced the embarrassment. All I'd wanted was to rent an impact wrench. Finally, he quoted me the rental fee and I turned around and walked out of the store, deciding to buy all the tools I would need at a competitor's store.

I ordered the wood I needed and had it delivered. Then I lugged each and every piece from the front yard, where they'd dropped it, to the back. I tried to be as discreet as possible. I was now embarrassed to let anyone know that I was attempting to build a deck all by myself. People would certainly have thought I was crazy. And what if I started the deck and couldn't finish it?

But I built the deck. Twenty feet long and eight feet wide, with access from the kitchen. It took several of my weekends and evenings, but when it was completed it was attractive and solid and I was proud of it. James was not talking to me and he remained unimpressed with my work.

In 1982, Serge was getting married and he wanted the wedding to be in our home. I decided it would be a good opportunity to add to the deck and so more weekends and evenings, along with vacation time, were spent expanding the deck to twelve feet in width and forty feet in length, adding access from the family room. It was now a 480 square-foot, redwood deck which ended up accommodating the wedding party nicely as guests mingled about, moving freely between the family room and kitchen and deck.

The wedding went well and I was proud of my son and new daughter-in-law. They made a beautiful couple. And I was proud of the outdoor arrangement and decoration. At one point I overheard James tell a guest that I had done all the work. "Would you believe she built this deck by herself?" He was proud, too. Everything looked perfect. And I was exhausted.

But as far as James and I went, things had been getting progressively worse. There was little affection. We had sex on occasion, but for my part it was perfunctory. I never felt loved. I felt empty. When all of the boys finally moved out of the house, I took another bedroom.

CHAPTER NINE
Sheba

~

ON AUGUST 29, 1982, A SUNDAY, I WAS SITTING OUT
on the deck with a cup of coffee, reading the paper and chat-
ting with Laura, Jacques' wife. Serge and Cindy's wedding
had been three weeks prior and everything was back to
normal at the house. The backyard and deck had been
stripped of the extra tables and umbrellas that we had rented
for the wedding and the house was clean and quiet. Jacques
and Laura were visiting for the day. Laura and I exchanged
sections of the local newspaper, the *Press Democrat.* I was in
the pet section and for whatever reason, my eyes happened
to catch a certain classified ad. AFGHAN HOUND PUPPIES
FOR SALE. I remembered the dog I had seen almost thirty
years before, on Barclay Avenue when Aldéma and I had
lived with his sister in Montréal. I was frightened of dogs,
but something about that one had affected me differently. It
was gentle and beautiful and long-haired and I had learned

that it was an Afghan hound. "Laura," I said, "let's go look at the puppies."

James and Jacques were watching television in the living room and declined our invitation to come along. Laura and I headed to Novato in Marin County, about ten miles south of Petaluma.

Jean Perlstein, the breeder of the hounds, welcomed us and led us to a large family room, making sure that all the doors were closed before she let the puppies in. The puppies were fourteen weeks old. Eight remained of the original litter of eleven and Laura and I watched as they played together on the floor. I knew nothing of the Afghan hound other what I had seen on the street in Montréal. They were adorable and carefree and I found myself mesmerized by them. With their long legs they looked more like baby lambs than the pudgy little puppies I had pictured in my mind. And they seemed just as fascinated by me and Laura, carefully coming over to me and walking around as we I sat on the floor with them, sniffing my back, my shoulders, my hair, and then coming around and sniffing my face. They moved around mostly as a group and if I made a sudden move, they'd all jump back at once.

The sire of the litter, Jean explained, was black and tan and an international champion, as were his sire and dam. The puppies' mother, a red brindle, though not a show dog, came from a long line of famous champions as well, going back to Stormhill Pandora and Shirkhan of Grandeur. This meant nothing to me. I had never even been to a dog show. But all that was about to change.

While her litter mates were playing, running around, and taking turns nudging me and Laura, a little red brindle came to me and sat on my lap. She leaned her little body heavily against my chest and stayed there without moving. It was strange. She watched her brothers and sisters continue to clown around but she never moved from her position, almost as though she were claiming me. When Laura and I eventually left, the little red brindle came with us.

Sheba, as I would name her, had started life with the odds stacked against her. She was the firstborn of the litter, but she had not been breathing, Jean would explain to me. The veterinarian supervising the birth had tried to induce her to breathe but ended up discarding her tiny body in a waste basket, giving up on her and turning his attention to the remaining ten puppies. Jean, checking and cleaning each puppy as it arrived, had heard a small whimper coming from behind her, coming from the waste basket, where, to her and the veterinarian's surprise, the little firstborn, against all likelihood, had been fighting for her breath, fighting for her life.

But now Sheba was strong and healthy. Jean had told me that she was well-structured by Afghan hound standards and, as is often the case with firstborns, had the potential to be a brilliant show dog. In fact, Jean had originally planned to keep her, but with eight puppies left for adoption, she let her go.

Jean was a responsible breeder, very organized. She had all the records ready in addition to instructions on how to raise Afghan puppies. I would learn, as I studied the breed, that the Afghan hound is not the right dog for everyone.

They're peaceful animals, but have special needs and demand lots of attention and maintenance. They're extremely sensitive to stress and can become sick to their stomachs, sometimes with severe digestive problems. But with the right person, the Afghan hound is a delightful and loving companion.

Though I knew nothing about the dog show world, I would soon find myself attracted to the idea. Jean would be there to help and guide me and Sheba and I would learn together. I began reading everything I could about the dog show business and I enrolled in conformation classes where the instructor encouraged me to show Sheba. "She's very 'houndy' looking," he said, "with a good stride, even for a puppy."

Weekends were now quality time with Sheba. We began to enter shows. Sheba loved every bit of it, sauntering proudly and holding her head up high in the various California show rings we'd travel to. Multiple times she won reserved winner and placed highly, most notably at the Afghan Hound Club Specialty competition where she competed against the very best.

Sheba was two when I received a call from Rose Upper, a friend of Jean's. Rose was another Afghan hound enthusiast who attended the shows regularly. Rose owned a motel in Santa Rosa, located right across the street from the Redwood Veterinary Clinic, a clinic Rose would eventually recommend to me.

"I rescued a puppy," Rose said on the phone. "And he's gorgeous. I think he'd be a good companion for Sheba. Why don't you come over and take a look at him?" Rose went on to explain that she'd taken the puppy from Marvin Johnson of Sebastopol, a disreputable breeder. The puppy had had pneumonia. Now healed, Johnson wanted the puppy back. But Rose had other plans, wanting to find a good home for the puppy instead.

When I arrived at Rose's I fell in love with the puppy as soon as I saw him. So did Sheba. The two were a great match. Canio was a blue domino, strikingly beautiful, and with excellent conformation. Like Sheba, he came from an impressive line of champions. He was the grandson of national and international champion Kabic the Challenger, nicknamed Pepsi, Best in Show of the 1983 Westminster Dog Show and the number one dog in the country that year.

From the time I brought Canio home, Sheba and he became inseparable. Canio had a way about him, facial expressions that ranged from displeasure to joy. He was a clown, always ready to entertain us. And he was clever. One day I was lying on the sofa and Canio decided the spot belonged to him. When barking and pushing at my feet didn't work, he ran to the back door, barking to let me know, ostensibly, that he needed to go out and pee. I got up from the sofa, slid the glass door open, and watched as Canio double-backed to the sofa, jumping on it and stretching his body out the full distance. I laughed, of course, and couldn't help but make a fuss about it. Canio understood immediately that he had done something special and it became a stunt he tried again and again.

With work and the dogs, I was busy and my life was full.

I was, for the most part, happy. Still, not a day went by that I didn't find myself thinking, on some level, about the little girl or the visions or what I'd said at Brookwood. Those things were always there.

But it was important for me to keep my mind occupied, to keep the thoughts at bay. It's not that I didn't necessarily want what was hidden to be revealed. It's more that I needed the revelations to come about slowly, manageably. I needed to be ready for them, even if I often wondered if the day when I would truly be ready would ever come. I mostly assumed I would probably die before knowing what it was that was buried so deep. And I became at peace with that.

Too, it was important for me to prove that I could function in society. That I was not crazy. To whom, I'm not sure. James. The boys. Very few people knew of my troubles. No one at work suspected, though they knew I could be very sensitive at times. Maybe I just felt I needed to prove it to myself.

CHAPTER TEN

Something Coming...Something Scary

~

AROUND 1984, MR. LEWIS RETIRED. I HAD WORKED under his management for approximately seven years. Interestingly, I'd learn much more about him after he retired. One evening in the early '90s, I found myself surprised to spot him in a movie I'd gone to the theater to see. He was in a crowd scene in *Sister Act* with Whoopi Goldberg. I called him afterwards, to let him know I'd seen him on the big screen. He was pleased that I called and he told me that he'd played small roles from time to time in several movies as well as a few television shows, like *The Streets of San Francisco.* A few years later I recognized him in the movie *True Crime.* He was sitting next to Clint Eastwood in a Petaluma bar called Washoe House.

A few times I ran into Mr. Lewis at the local grocery store and he always stopped to talk. One day I read in the newspaper that his wife died and I felt sad for Mr. Lewis, knowing that they had been very dedicated to each other. She was an opera singer. Mr. Lewis himself died in April of 2011. He was eighty-eight. Reading his obituary, I learned that he'd enlisted in the Army Air Corps in 1942 and served in World War II as well as the Korean War.

At any rate, a new store manager came in to replace Mr. Lewis back in '84. Larry Stuart was heavy, with curly reddish hair and a ruddy complexion. He was anxious to make a good impression with the staff, but that seemed to mean cracking jokes, often uncomfortably crude ones. Mr. Lewis had always been so professional with us. Stuart could be abrasive. The store's coffee shop manager, a woman raising a daughter by herself often came into my office crying because of Stuart. Once she said that Stuart told her she needed to lose weight. And that she needed to have her teeth fixed. "It's disgusting for the customers to see while they're eating," he had said to her. "Get your teeth fixed or find another job." And he'd said it in front of others. Stuart liked to have an audience when he displayed his authority.

Where Stuart learned his management skills, I never knew. But in those days, men were selected for management over women. With Stuart there were sexual comments. And he would improperly touch subordinates. Once he came into my office and asked me to scratch his back, in front of my staff. When I reported an obscene phone call I received one afternoon he thought it was funny. "Well, tell your boyfriend to stop calling," he laughed, a joke I heard him repeat to other employees.

He made racist comments, too, and in my time at J.C.

Penney, I heard more of those than I had ever heard back in Pennsylvania. Michael Jackson was popular at the time but Stuart refused to carry any merchandise promoting him. We carried John Travolta merchandise instead. Whenever a black person would enter the store, he'd instruct someone to follow her. A catalog customer came in once with her five-year-old grandson and Stuart had her trailed all around the store.

"You don't need to do that," I protested. "She's a good customer. And a very nice person."

"She might be nice," he retorted, "but her grandson is a little thief."

Soon, I dreaded going to work. I started feeling tense and anxious. Before long, I once again felt my control over my life slowly slipping. And I felt something else. Something was coming toward me, though I had no idea what. I felt tense and afraid. I knew it was something important. Something scary.

Whatever it was, it created a turmoil inside of me that made my life difficult. My concentration slipped to a low point. I had trouble working and forced myself every day to try to stay in control. I felt threatened. Suddenly, I couldn't be alone in the house without feeling tremendous fear, of what I could not say. But I began to keep the knives off the kitchen counter, burying them in drawers, and hiding a butcher block in the pantry, keeping it out of sight.

I could not sleep. At night, I would curl up in bed and I would cry and think of the song about Jonah and the whale and silently sing as I had sung in my childhood, the song that had comforted me so. *Jonah dans la baleine disait je voudrais m'en aller, bo-boum bo-boum.* I wanted to run away.

One morning in October 1985, the news was full of a story about a humpback whale that had lost his way and had swum into the San Francisco Bay. After a few days in the bay, the whale, nicknamed Humphrey by the media, swam on towards the Sacramento River. I couldn't help but wonder if somehow Humphrey had heard my silent cries. Years later, something similar would happen. A wayward gray whale would swim up from San Pablo Bay and navigate up the Petaluma River, nearly reaching downtown Petaluma. I went and saw her two miles from my house and again I wondered how very strange it seemed. Somehow it was comforting to think that the whales had come so close to me.

With the situation at work and my increasing loss of control, I felt, for the first time in several years, the need for counseling. By then, James's family health insurance coverage had gone to an HMO health plan and I set up an appointment with my primary care physician Dr. Andrew so he could refer me to a psychologist. I liked Dr. Andrew. It turned out that his father was born in Canada and worked for J.C. Penney after moving to the U.S. Dr. Andrew was kind and somewhat protective of me, and I felt as though I could speak freely to him. He always seemed relaxed and composed and his presence was calming to me. I didn't reveal everything to Dr. Andrew but he had a sense I was, perhaps, heading for a breakdown. He recommended Dr. Ann Rivo, a Marin County psychologist and I went to see her for the first time on September 24, 1985, and then every other week for the next two months.

I spoke with Rivo mostly about my troubles at work and also about my past—what I could remember of it. Rivo was concerned. I would ultimately learn that she would diagnose me with multiple personality disorder, though I don't think I mentioned the seven-year-old or the twelve-year-old. Apparently I would come across to her in different ways during different visits—very intelligent and coherent one day, hardly able to form words another.

It was good that I had someone to talk to. Like Jim Fraser, Ann Rivo was thoughtful and caring. But when I asked her, she confessed that she had never before treated anyone with repressed memory. Ann could not provide the help I needed.

And then on November 20, I was back in Dr. Andrew's waiting room for a routine checkup. There were other offices there for other doctors and the shared waiting room was full of patients. I was anxious, afraid of something happening with me that would embarrass me in front of everybody. But though I didn't think of it this way at the time, it was a very safe place for me to be—a doctor's waiting room with other people around. And looking back, maybe that's why it arrived just then. Maybe that was the perfect place. For as I sat, staring off into space, waiting for Dr. Andrew, I suddenly felt a soothing, peaceful calm passing through my body, followed in moments by another vision, like a still picture. Clear and unmistakable. The calm, having come upon me as if to help me absorb the blow, dissipated slowly as I realized the meaning of the picture and I soon felt myself in a panic as I grasped the vision: A basement with a dirt floor. A mound of fresh dirt. A body underneath.

I understood what it meant. The basement was from our house in Lac-Mégantic. The body was mine. I was seven years old. My father had killed me, or at least he thought that he had. And then he had buried me alive.

C H A P T E R   E L E V E N
The Basement

~

I COULD FEEL MY HEART POUNDING AGAINST MY RIBS and I felt a sinking sensation, as if my blood was being drained from my body and I thought I was going to faint. Surely, I thought, the people in the waiting room could tell something was wrong with me. I needed to get out. I left the waiting area and walked hurriedly to the restroom. I felt panicky, fearful of coming completely unglued. I needed to keep myself together. In the restroom I splashed water on my face and on the back of my neck. I took some deep breaths and steadied myself as best I could, then returned to my chair.

Dr. Andrew himself came to get me from the waiting room when it was my turn. As we walked to his office I told him I had just had a vision of what had happened to me when I was seven. I couldn't tell him what it was but he could clearly see I was distraught. He patted me on the shoulder and said, "Now, doesn't that feel better to get rid of those old memories?" It was an odd thing to say but later I would remind myself that Dr. Andrew was not a psychiatrist; he could not have known what I was going through or what the right thing to say would have been. But his detached reaction had, at least, the effect of sobering me enough to where I could drive safely back home.

Loneliness greeted me when I walked into the house, falling on me like a blanket as I took a seat on the recliner by the fireplace. The room seemed dark and eerily quiet. My mind was racing with forty-year-old memories. I could not displace the vision of the grave in the basement. I thought of calling Dr. Rivo, but wondered, what's the use? I began to pray, begging God not to abandon me. But by then, I felt that God was throwing more at me than I could possibly handle. If He was giving me a mission, I prayed, the least He could do was give me the tools to work with, and not just pile trauma after trauma on top of me. I was losing my faith. I felt alone, but for Canio and Sheba.

When James came home from work, he glanced into the living room to see me sitting in the chair and then continued to walk down the hallway into the kitchen. By that time, he had completely lost patience with me and my problems. *Here we go again*, he probably thought, seeing me frozen in the chair. I could hear him in the kitchen getting some ice cream from the freezer and a bowl from the cupboard. Then I could hear the spoon hitting the bowl as he ate. When he was finished I watched him walk upstairs. He never once looked back at me. Later he went out and came back with a McDonald's hamburger and fries. And then he went to bed, having said not a word to me the entire evening.

The next morning James went to work, once again looking quickly over at me as he walked towards the door and, once again, saying nothing. The day went by with me slowly dozing off from time to time, taking comfort in sleep. When James returned that afternoon, he went straight to his bedroom. A couple of hours later, Jacques and Serge stopped by the house. I was very glad to see them and we talked and I confided in them the vision I had had the day before at the doctor's office. They listened attentively and we talked some more. They asked if I'd eaten. No, I said, I was not hungry. And then they said they wanted to check in with their father and they went upstairs. In a little while, all three came down.

"Mom," Serge said, "let's get out of the house and go for a drive." I felt better having opened up to Serge and Jacques and the idea of going out appealed to me. It felt heartening to know they were willing to spend the time to take me for a drive. Perhaps we would go to dinner someplace. But in the car I suddenly realized we were heading to Marin.

"Where are we going?" I asked.

"There's a nice house in Marin we want you to see," said Serge.

Soon we pulled up to the entrance of Marin General Hospital. "What are we doing here?" I said.

"C'mon, Mom," Jacques said and I followed them dutifully inside. We sat in the waiting room for probably a half hour to forty-five minutes. I looked from James to Jacques to Serge, but they would look away. Nobody said a thing. I knew then that I was under observation. Eventually two officers came into the waiting room and escorted me outside where a paddy wagon had pulled up. I climbed obediently into the back and sat on a bench. Before they closed the doors, I saw Serge outside and I extended my arms to him. "*Please...*" I uttered, but they shut the doors.

I could not blame Jacques and Serge, though I felt somewhat betrayed by them, especially by Jacques in whom I had confided back when we had gone to Mickle the first time. But I knew I was more of a stranger to my sons at that point than a mother. My problems, now going back years, back to when Jacques and Serge and Alain and Danny lived with us, created a dysfunctional family atmosphere the dynamics of which continued to impact my relationships with my sons. We were all affected in one way or another by what had been happening to me. Taking me, unwillingly, to the hospital was what Jacques and Serge imagined to be the best course of action, bolstered by the encouragement of James, of course. And I had no means by which to argue otherwise.

The paddy wagon drove across the street and pulled up in front of the red brick façade of Ross Valley Psychiatric Hospital and I was helped out of the back and led inside. All the while I remained calm. I didn't argue with anyone or resist the officers. I knew if I resisted, if I tried to fight, or run, or even raise my voice, that would be all the excuse the medical staff would need to handcuff me or force drugs into me.

Soon I felt hungry and dehydrated and I couldn't remember when I'd eaten last. A hospital attendant led me to my room and handed me a glass of water. And then some pills.

"I don't take medications," I said. "I've had severe reactions to them in the past. A sleeping pill might be okay. What I would really like is some food."

"You'll need to take the pills," she insisted. "They're good for you."

"No, I can take a mild sleeping pill but not psychiatric medication. I'm tired and I'm hungry and I need to talk to someone." Then out of the corner of my eye I saw two aides suddenly appear, a man and a woman. One held a syringe. "No, please...please. I'll take the pills. Please!" But they grabbed me and pushed me face down onto the bed. I felt my panties being pulled down and the needle entering my skin. They were quick and efficient. They turned me over in one fluid motion and I heard the straps hit the underside of the bed and the click of the buckles. They spoke to each other the whole time but never said a word to me. And then in an instant, they were out of the room and I was left all alone. I tried to slide out of the restraints but it was futile.

Soon I was overcome by terror and grief. I closed my eyes and tried to remain calm, but I could not control my fear or the trembling of my body. Suddenly, the vision of the little girl came into my mind, as clear as it had ever been, and I knew at once what she'd felt, tied to the bed, and I felt a connection to her I had never before experienced. I wept for her before losing consciousness.

When I awoke the next day, I felt nothing. By then the straps had been removed. My face was twitching and grimacing. My mouth was dry and contorted, my vision blurry. More drugs had been injected into my body while

I'd been unconscious. My tongue would not stay in my mouth and I had to push it in with my fingers when I tried to talk, but I felt no embarrassment. I felt no emotion at all. I was experiencing what I would come to learn was EPS—extrapyramidal symptoms—a condition induced by the Thorazine that had been used, a condition that can sometimes be irreversible. Most likely they had used too much. I was small, after all, and medications had always had a strong effect on me. Plus, I hadn't eaten. The Thorazine had been given to me on an empty stomach.

My chemical straitjacket lasted several hours.

I slept some more and when I awoke again I saw a blurry figure of a man sitting by the window. "Good morning," the blurry figure said. "I'm Doctor Knepfer, your doctor."

"I've never seen you before. I want to go home."

"You told Dr. Mickle that you had repressed memories when you were hospitalized before." I said nothing. "It's not true, is it?"

I told him to leave my room and then refused to say anything more to him. After a while, he rose and walked out.

As the drugs began to wear off, the enormity of the situation struck me. I was terrified. I wondered if they would stop me if I tried to leave and I walked out of my room and began walking down the hallway toward a back patio. At a certain point an alarm sounded, set off by a motion detector. I turned and walked back toward my room. There would be no leaving.

Rather than risk being forced drugs and tied to the bed again, I gave up. Obediently, I took the oral drugs they handed me. Without a word of protest I let them inspect my mouth to ensure the drugs had gone down my throat. I became a very good patient—a model prisoner. The world, it seemed to me, had been turned upside down. Murderers were let out of prisons. Wife beaters and child abusers went unpunished. And I, who had never been a threat to anyone in her life, whose only sin was the harboring of wounds that ran deep and unbridled, was a prisoner that, like a violent criminal, needed restraining. If this was sanity, I thought, then I'd rather be mad.

I waited them out.

I was held at Ross Valley for three days. During that time I was administered a regular regimen of medication. Dr. Knepfer wanted to hold me longer (I supposed James's insurance coverage was satisfactory) but the panel of doctors at the hospital voted for my release. Knepfer released me with prescribed drugs and prescriptions for more drugs, writing in my dossier that if I refused to take them, shots would be "made available" for me. I needed the drugs, he wrote, to function in life.

I left the hospital a fragmented soul. The fresh air hit my face as I walked out. I heard birds singing. Screams were choking me and burning in my throat but I allowed neither the screams nor sobs to pass my lips. I walked rapidly, afraid to look back and afraid to look ahead. Every person seemed suspicious, every person seemed as if they might grab me and drag me back into the hospital. I began to run but caught myself. Could they throw me in jail for running? I wondered. What if I cried? Can they lock me away if

I cry on the street?

When I got home, I flushed the drugs down the toilet and tore up the prescriptions. I knew I had to get a hold of myself and take control. If not, I would go back to Ross Valley and I felt that the next time I would not come out alive. Detoxification from the drugs ended up being less painful than recovery from the trauma of forced hospitalization.

In about a week my head cleared and I soon went back to work. I was on my own. I knew that. And I was scared. But the hospital stay made me stronger and all the more determined to survive, to learn how to live with all that was visiting me from my past. I had come to understand that I was a victim of trauma, a trauma from long ago that was nevertheless an integral part of my present. And the hospitalization persuaded me in no uncertain terms that the experts did not understand trauma victims. I would have to take responsibility for my own treatment.

In December I called my mother. She knew I'd been hospitalized. My family back in Canada knew I'd been having problems. But I'd never spoken to my mother about it before. I asked her about a particular weekend from my childhood. I was seven. I seemed to remember she had gone away for several days, to the States with her mother, my Grandmother Brault, to a funeral of a relative. It was the fall of 1942. It was the only time I could ever remember my mother going away anywhere. We had been left with our father and our Grandmother Drouin.

"I need to know what happened when you went away to

the funeral," I said. "Father beat me almost to death, didn't he?"

Mother's voice broke almost to a whisper and I could tell she knew exactly what I was referring to. "Your father," she began, "had waitresses working for him at the restaurant."

I made her stop. It was obviously painful for her to talk about and I did not want to hear any more. In my mind, things too quickly began falling into place. My mother was about to confirm what I had been suspecting for a long time. I knew about the waitresses working at the restaurant and I knew that my father drank at times. On that night from long ago, I must have heard someone in the house. Had my father brought a waitress home? Noises from his bedroom in the middle of the night—did I go in and investigate, thinking, perhaps, that my mother had come home? I had apparently interrupted my father and in his drunken rage, he had chased me and thrown me down to the basement. I remembered the dirt floor, the furnace, the cords of wood. I tried to find a place to hide, but there was nowhere to go.

I didn't want to talk about the basement.

"I was lying on a bed," I told my mother on the phone. A bedroom had been the next thing that I had remembered after the basement. "And there was a chair by the door and a window and boxes of something in the room."

"Sewing material," Mother said. "Yes, you were in the maid's room. The maid was gone for the weekend so they took you to the maid's room."

"And there was a priest in the room."

"Monsignor Bonin."

"Yes, Monsignor Bonin." I sat quietly, not knowing what to say or what to ask. Perhaps I had heard enough for the time being.

"Your father told me he was sorry, Marcelle," my mother said at last. "He said he was sorry. Your father was very sorry." At that, I suddenly remembered sitting next to my mother as a child, hearing her say that Father had cried and told her he was sorry. He had never said it to me.

A few days after my call to Mother, I received a letter in the mail from one of my brothers. "Why are you asking our mother about these things?" he wrote. "She is extremely upset, Marcelle. Extremely upset. Please don't talk to her about these things anymore."

Shortly after that, my mother had a minor stroke, losing vision in one eye. When I next spoke to her on the phone I asked if she thought that what we had talked about had played a part in the stroke. "Probably," she said.

I never spoke to my mother again about what happened that weekend. But I eventually came to the realization that the Monsignor would have been in the maid's room for only one reason: to administer the last sacrament. The vision of my grave was real. I knew it to be so. My father had beaten me or, more likely, choked me, almost to death. Perhaps, for a few moments, I was dead. My father had thought so. In his drunken panic, he had dug in the dirt of the basement, making a shallow grave that I had somehow seen from above. This of course explained my horrified reaction during my first stay at Ross Valley eight years earlier when one of the patients began digging in the ground with a small hand shovel. How I escaped the grave, I do not know, nor is it likely that I will ever know. But I was apparently carried upstairs to the maid's room where the priest was called. I don't remember hearing the last sacrament but in thinking about the maid's room one day, I suddenly remembered Monsignor Bonin talking to me after I had apparently resumed consciousness. "Marcelle," he had said, *"tu dois oublier, mon enfant, et de ne jamais parler de ça encore. Tu dois oublier tout."*

"You have to forget, my child, and never speak of it again. You have to forget everything."

CHAPTER TWELVE
Protector

∼

THERE WAS ONE THING MORE MY MOTHER HAD TOLD me during our telephone conversation in December of 1985. I had asked about the other vision. The first one, the one that had always been with me. The little girl tied to the bed, the nun, the upside down votive candles.

"You were very sick, Marcelle," my mother had told me. "Of course you were in the boarding school at the time." She hesitated a moment and added, "Yes, I seem to remember that the nun told me they used the procedure to cure a very bad chest cold."

Years later I would infer from my brothers and sisters why we had been sent to the Catholic boarding school, though no one provided any definitive detail. When my mother had returned home from that funeral in 1942, there were some terrible quarrels between her and my father. I had asked about it before. Back in 1976, I had called my sister

Louise to ask about Mother's return from the funeral. Obviously significant to me, I hadn't, of course, made a connection in my mind at the time between Mother's return and the basement. But Louise, only four at the time of the funeral, remembered very well Father being terrifyingly violent towards our mother. He had wanted to kill her. Since '76, I hadn't pursued the matter any further. I had put it away and the thoughts of Father's anger remained buried until the vision at Dr. Andrew's office brought the memories to the surface.

And in time, I remembered being outside, hiding behind a post from our swing set. Father was coming my way and I was terrified. *You had better keep your mouth shut,* he said grimly and I remember feeling that if I did not obey him, it would mean my life. From my siblings I would learn that our father had beaten our mother very badly. Did I tell my mother about the basement? Had she then confronted my father? Was I responsible for my mother's beating?

Very shortly after that day, my sisters and I were all sent to the boarding school, even four-year-old Louise. I can only guess that my mother could not care for us at that time. The boarding school was the school we were already attending, but now we were to live there. We didn't even come home for Christmas that year, although I have a recollection of being taken to Sherbrooke just around Christmas for surgery to have my appendix removed. I don't remember how I got there. I remember being in the hospital because the staff was organizing a Christmas play and I almost got picked to be in the play but apparently I was the wrong girl.

And I have a glimpse of being on the train with my father and a recollection that I was certain we were going back home. But I was delivered back to the boarding school. I can imagine that my heart must have been heavy but back then children did not question authority. We simply obeyed.

In the boarding school, then, I had most likely become ill as my mother recalled. A serious chest cold. It was an archaic remedy, perhaps brought to the boarding house by a couple of nuns who had recently arrived from France. The convent, *Les Soeurs de la Congrégation de Notre Dame,* had originally been an order established in France and it was not unusual to have nuns coming in from France in those days.

The remedy involves candles lit in jars and then extinguished. The jars are quickly placed upside down on the afflicted area of the body—the chest in my case. A vacuum is thus created and the jars act as suction cups, supposedly drawing blood to the area to promote healing. The practice is called cupping.

I only learned this years later, researching desperately in order to discover the meaning of the bizarre memory. By turns I had considered that what I had seen in the vision was either some exorcism ritual, or some rite for the dead, the latter especially because I'd become certain the girl was not alive. Since learning of the arcane therapy, I determined the prospect must have been exceedingly frightening to me at the time. I had just been traumatized beyond comprehension by my father. Buried alive. I must have fought back. I must have fought against the nun who, in turn, must have tied my hands to the headboard. This, then, explained my otherwise baffling reaction to the nun who had sat down by my bed when I had been in the hospital to deliver Daniel. So terrified was I in the boarding school infirmary that I disconnected from the seven-year-old girl, resulting in the out-of-body experience that enabled me to see the girl and to come to assume she was dead.

We remained separated, she and I, and it would take thirty-five years before I realized we were one and the same person. And yet, in a sense, we remained apart.

Over time, I came to marvel at what my mind had done in order to allow the seven-year-old to survive. My instinctive ability to dissociate wasn't mental illness. It was a survival technique born of necessity. It was a gift. Naturally, it would not have been recognized as such by the psychiatric profession which chooses instead to broad-brush labels upon those who might have trouble sorting things out for themselves, frequently retreating back to their preferred solution for such traumatized people: mind-numbing medication.

Since being strapped to the bed at Ross Valley, I had begun to deeply sympathize with the seven-year-old girl. I wanted to help her, to nurture her. I wanted to get closer to her. This would ultimately be made easier in large part by the gradual softening of the twelve-year-old who, I came to realize, was in place as a means by which to keep me from the younger girl, to keep me from the memories, to keep me from forcing the seven-year-old to relive her trauma. Something else, I imagine, that my mind had set up as a way to prevent me from learning the truth until I could better accept it. To bring it upon me in a slow, measured way.

As the older girl was loosening her protective grip on the younger girl, the dogs were helping in the process. Prior to the vision at Dr. Andrew's office of the grave in the basement, I would often come home from work for lunch. Alone in the house I felt fear and anxiety, even anger and hostility. So much so that I'd come in through the front door and pass directly through the house to the backyard without stopping. Sheba and Canio would follow me outside.

There, in the backyard, I began to teach the twelve-year-old girl to feel. I would let her touch Canio and feel his soft coat and pet him and hug him. I know she felt it. I know that for the first time she was willing to give me a chance and trust me and little by little, this had an effect on both girls. The gentleness of the dogs seemed to calm them and soothe them because gradually I began to feel the anger and hostility dissipate. The dogs, that is to say, calmed and soothed *me*. And allowed me a safe place from which to consider myself at seven. That was, perhaps, the net effect, anyway. But for me it wasn't so neat. For me, it was two distinct personalities—a twelve-year-old girl acting as protector for the seven-year-old girl. Soon, as I felt the anger decrease, I no longer feared that someone was trying to take over, at least for the time being.

To understand the strength of the girls I had to think of the time and place in which they lived and recognize the importance of the Catholic faith to our family and to most of the population in the area. Monsignor Bonin, who gave me the last sacrament in 1942, was a widely respected priest and he left a tremendous impression on the girls. "You have to forget, my child", he had said. It was a command that even an adult would not dare violate for fear of heavenly repercussion. Monseigneur Bonin died in 1944 and his name continued to live long after his death. There were buildings named after him.

I kept busy. The dogs helped all three of us. In 1986, I decided to breed Canio and Sheba. It was a difficult decision to make. Afghan hounds were known to deliver large litters. What if Sheba had eleven or twelve puppies? How would I deal with them all? I hesitated for a long time. It wouldn't be until almost a year after my forced stay at Ross Valley that I would decide to go ahead with the breeding, feeling ultimately that the puppies would be a way to further tame the twelve-year-old and calm the seven-year-old.

Sheba was four and Canio two. I was determined to make it a well-planned breeding. Both before and after the pregnancy the dogs were tested and very closely monitored by our veterinarian. Sheba, in fact, would be the first dog in Sonoma County to benefit from the use of a sonogram machine, a new tool at the clinic. From the sonogram we learned that Sheba was expecting just two puppies, extremely rare for the Afghan hound. And I thought of the two girls for whom I had originated the breeding idea.

Sheba went into labor on Sunday morning December 21, 1986. She slept on my bed and I recognized right away the signs. I rushed her to the emergency hospital immediately as I had been instructed by the veterinarian. The puppies were too large to risk a natural birth.

Sheba came through the cesarean procedure just fine. The puppies were beautiful and healthy, both females—one a black-and-tan and one a blue brindle domino. Sheba was red brindle and Canio a blue domino.

I nicknamed the little black-and-tan Mika and the blue brindle domino Evita. The dog registration protocol in the dog show world is that you register the dog with the breeder's kennel name first, then you can name your dog what you want. As I was the breeder, I used the name Mégantic. The puppy's American Kennel Club registered names would be Mégantic's Little Sparrow and Mégantic's Little Evita. For some reason it seemed important that they had a connection to my hometown.

Mika, the little black-and-tan, almost met a tragic end within a few hours of her birth. When I came to the clinic to pick the puppies up, I found Mika with a cord from a torn towel, used as bedding material, wrapped tightly around her neck. She was frantically fighting for breath. An attendant rushed in with a pair of scissors and cut the towel. Mika recovered, but the incident proved an omen of tragedy to come.

For the time being, though, the house was bursting with life. Sheba, Canio, Mika, and Evita filled my home with delight. And I felt a profound love coming from within. The girls loved the puppies.

Just four weeks after giving birth, Sheba became violently ill. My regular veterinarian Dr. Popkin was out of town, but I took Sheba to the same clinic where another veterinarian examined her. "She's fine," assured Dr. Skinner after a brief examination and I could sense that he felt he was dealing with an overprotective owner. But I accepted his instructions to withhold food and water from Sheba for twenty-four hours and to administer Darbazine for the vomiting. He was an older, more experienced vet than Dr. Popkin, after all.

The following day Sheba was still vomiting. The medication was rendered useless as Sheba could not keep it down. She was weak and dehydrated when I took her back to the clinic. I didn't have a lot of experience in canine medical illness, but it seemed pretty clear to me that Sheba was very ill. Again, Skinner examined her. I explained that although I had withheld food and water for twenty-four hours, as directed, Sheba had urinated frequently and was still vomiting. Once again, Skinner found nothing wrong with her.

"I'll inject her with some barium and you can bring her back tomorrow morning for an x-ray," he said, as if to placate me, and I wondered if he thought that maybe I'd brought Sheba to the clinic as some warped way to get attention, the way you sometimes hear of parents doing so with their kids. But I often had difficulty trusting my intuition. Was I imagining that Sheba was ill? This was a professional, educated man. An experienced and trained veterinarian. Certainly he would know.

I left with Sheba slowly following me out of the clinic. I stayed up with her all night. She vomited most of the barium that had been pumped into her stomach and made countless trips outside to relieve herself. She drank water, too—large quantities of it. Later I would learn what all her symptoms pointed to; Sheba had diabetes brought on by her pregnancy.

The next morning, when I brought Sheba to Sonoma County Emergency Veterinary Clinic she was highly dehydrated and in severe diabetic shock. I told Dr. Blaine, a visiting doctor at the clinic about Sheba's history. He was able to diagnose her immediately with diabetes. Blood tests confirmed his diagnosis. "If Sheba survives this," Dr. Blaine told me, "she'll need close supervision and insulin shots for the rest of her life." Then he paused and said, "Most people would euthanize their dog."

"No," I told him. "I'll take care of her. I want to save her. Please." Sheba spent several days hospitalized and Dr. Blaine took x-rays to document the barium in Sheba's stomach. He thought it was outrageous and he encouraged me to file a complaint with the Veterinary Medicine Board of Examiners.

Sheba came home. And it was to a joyous reunion with her four-week-old puppies. She ran to them, pulling me along as I held on to her leash. She smelled them, licked them, turned them over, and gave each a full inspection. They cried happily. And so did I.

The puppies grew. But in early March 1987, I was in the backyard with all four dogs when I heard an awful cry from one of the puppies. Mika was holding her paw up and she looked at me for help. Dr. Popkin was out of town again and I visited two local veterinarians. One insisted that Mika was being a crybaby and would be just fine in the morning. She was not fine in the morning. She walked on three paws and cried if she tried to use her right paw. The next veterinarian took an x-ray at a wrong angle and missed what was a broken bone. The day after that, Dr. Popkin was back in and he x-rayed Mika's paw to discover the break. Mika wore a soft cast that had to be replaced weekly due to her growing bones.

In April of 1987, Little Evita needed surgery to repair an umbilical hernia, something the vet discovered when he first examined her. "Routine," was how Dr. Popkin described the procedure. But afterwards, when I picked Evita up, she let out a loud yap in the parking lot. Clearly she was hurting and I turned to take her back in. Then I caught myself. Would they think I was just being overprotective? I took her home.

Evita went to sleep when we returned to the house but before long she awoke, crying out in intense pain. I ran to her and could see that her stomach had opened at the suture line; her insides were protruding through. I rushed her to the emergency hospital where Dr. Blaine, the same doctor who had saved Sheba's life just a few months earlier, examined Evita in disbelief.

What Dr. Popkin had done, explained Dr. Blaine, was simply open the outer layer skin of the stomach, put one stitch in the fat edge of the hernia, and then close the outer skin with two stitches. As Evita began to move, the inner stitch tore off the fat and her insides started pushing at the outer opening. The pain for Little Evita must have been excruciating. It was surgery at its worst. Dr. Blaine wrote up a report and encouraged me to file a complaint. Then he fixed the botched surgery, doing it properly—twenty sutures to close the two overlapping layers in an alternating pattern and nylon monofilament to close the outer skin. Little Evita would survive.

I found these cases of neglect very strange. Were these cases of malpractice exceptions, or were they the standard in the veterinary community? I wrote a letter to the editor of a local paper, the *Argus Courier*, asking the same question. A veterinarian from Healdsburg responded with outrage. *How dare I?* he asked. I also contacted the *Press Democrat* and talked to Jim Sweeney, one of their writers. Here were stories of veterinary malpractice that surely the public would be interested in. But Jim wouldn't bite.

Around July of that year, I started to notice that Sheba was bumping into furniture as she walked in unfamiliar places. And I noticed that she followed Canio very closely in the backyard, something that was unusual for her; Canio normally followed Sheba. Sheba was losing her sight and the loss was rapid. But she adapted well. We made sure not to move the furniture around so that she had a familiar path through the house. Canio seemed to have a sense for the situation and he became very protective of Sheba.

Meanwhile, I continued to work at J.C. Penney until September, 1987. Eventually, I could take Larry Stuart no more. The final straw was a series of sick jokes he kept making about a convicted rapist and torturer whose parole in California had made national front page news. I was dumbfounded that such a man could be in charge of a store. I spoke to James about it. "Ignore him," he told me—the same impractical advice he had given me when I was working for Paul at Host International.

Finally, I found myself at a point where I had to make a decision. I liked my job. I needed to work. But I was constantly at the edge of panic and felt as though I was losing the battle. My home life was crumbling with anxiety about the dogs and the veterinary malpractice. I could have survived and worked through all of it had I not had Stuart's constant harassment to contend with. I felt as if I could not survive with both home and work collapsing around me. I went to the personnel office and announced that I'd had enough. "I'm going home," I said. I was angry. I should not have been the one to lose my job. At the time, my department had a twenty-one percent growth in revenue over the previous year. I had a good and dedicated staff. I felt proud of my department, but I was tired and needed a break.

In a few days, the personnel manager called wanting to know when I was coming back to work. "I'm not," I said. Almost immediately I regretted it. I went back to Stuart and told him all I really wanted was some time off. He wouldn't listen. I was out of a job. I spoke with Mr. Lewis, my former manager, and he suggested that I contact the district manager. But the district manager sided with Stuart.

In addition to losing my position, I had been two weeks short of being vested with the company. I had worked for J.C. Penney for two weeks shy of ten years. I was going to lose my profit sharing. I went to see an attorney and James accompanied me. The attorney was interested. J.C. Penney was a big company. He spoke to several other employees and found evidence of sexual harassment and racial discrimination, as well as simply bad management skills on Stuart's part. Most of the employees supported me; they'd had problems with Stuart as well. To show how Stuart had affected me, I gave permission for Ann Rivo and Ross Valley to release their files to the attorney.

But then the attorney effectively abandoned me when the state of California passed at-will employment legislation. Outside of termination for such things as race or sex or religion, and a small number of other exceptions, an employee could be fired for basically any reason. We didn't have a case. I requested the attorney's file on me and it was then that I read my medical report from Ross Valley and what Rivo had written about me—the multiple personality disorder. She had never told me what I had already known.

Without an attorney, I called the J.C. Penney attorney myself, explaining my predicament, my potential loss of profit sharing because of two weeks. J.C. Penney agreed to release the profit sharing I had earned. It was a help, but I was still out of a job. It was devastating. The store had been my home for ten years. I had made good friends there and the work had been good for me. Leaving felt a little bit like dying.

I felt lost and I almost gave up. Maybe, I thought to myself, I should return home to Canada.

CHAPTER THIRTEEN

Feral

∼

THE PROBLEM WITH RETURNING TO CANADA WAS THAT it was no longer my home. Not really. But neither was the United States. I felt unwelcomed here. In addition to the job loss and the inability to get anyone to help me with my repressed memories, I felt like a stranger in Petaluma.

When we first moved to Petaluma in 1974, I used to shop downtown and, walking along the streets, I would often notice bumper stickers: *Welcome to California—Now Go Home.* This stayed with me and after a while I was sure they really meant: *Welcome to Petaluma—Now Go Home.* Too, the sentiment seemed expressed pretty clearly by the attitude of the downtown merchants and their workers. I stopped shopping downtown. So did a lot of non-native residents. The attitude changed probably in the early 1990s when the businesses decided they wanted our money. But by then we were all accustomed to driving to Rohnert Park,

Santa Rosa, and Marin County to shop.

Working for J.C. Penney had been good for my morale and gave me self-confidence. I felt a part of the community and it was good. But there had been many occasions when I became self-conscious of my French-Canadian accent. I spoke as little as I could. I hated my accent, hated the way I had to sometimes struggle for the right word. I studied and practiced my vocabulary and diction as best I could, but the accent never left me and I always felt judged because of it. I could see it in people's eyes. And people would also make racist comments in front of me, unaware that I was married to a black man.

All these thoughts came crashing in on me after losing my job at J.C. Penney and I wasted weeks feeling sorry for myself and angry at myself for my inability to deal with the store manager. He should have left—not me. I should have done something about it before it came to the point that I couldn't handle the situation anymore. The thoughts made me feel worse and I just wanted to run away from it all.

I had assumed that by then that I had lost my Canadian citizenship, that I was essentially a person without a country. I called the Canadian embassy to ask what I needed to return to Canada and was relieved to learn that I possessed dual citizenship. I could return anytime I wanted. My spirits were boosted a little to learn that I had a choice. But I didn't really want to return to Canada. I decided I didn't want to run away ever again. And how could I know that things would be any better for me there? And I knew nobody outside of Lac-Mégantic and I was not going to return to

Lac-Mégantic. I would have been a stranger in Canada and, in the end, I decided to stay, feeling at least somewhat empowered by the available option, even if I was, looking back, perhaps never completely serious about exercising it.

Still, I was feeling helpless and close to losing control once again. I knew I could not lose control. Losing control meant Ross Valley. And Ross Valley would mean death for me, if not literally so, then certainly for my spirit, my freedom. I knew that my next stay at Ross Valley could well be a permanent one. I needed a plan. I needed to keep my mind clear. I needed work. That was first and foremost. I needed to provide for myself, and more than anything, I needed to keep focused and busy.

In December of 1987, three months after I left J.C. Penney, I went to work at Barlas Feeds Store. I had gone there one day to buy food for the dogs. Jean Perlstein had recommended the place. Barlas Feeds was a family-owned operation. They sold pet food and animal feed and the property was a sprawling country setting with feed silos that held corn and wheat, and a large hay-stocked barn. At the back of the property was the truck repair shop and beyond that were a few barns rented out to a chicken farmer. Towards the front of the property, about four-hundred feet from the road, was the main office, which also housed the pet food as well as an assortment of medications for various farm animals.

I stood in the office at the customer counter and overheard Ann Barlas on the phone telling someone that they were looking for help. "I didn't mean to eavesdrop," I said when she hung up, "but I happen to be looking for a job."

"Well," she said, "you must know about pet foods since you're here for your dog. What do you know about farm animal feeds?"

"Not a thing," I answered, "but I can learn."

"What do you think, Leon?" she asked her husband whose glass-enclosed office was directly across the counter. Leon Barlas waved me in and asked a few questions about my background. He and Ann were both in their early eighties and I would learn that the business had been in the family for ninety years. I assured Leon I had good customer skills and that I was dependable, and I offered to fill out an application.

"That won't be necessary. What kind of salary are you looking for?"

"Well, I was making $8.60 an hour at J.C. Penney. I wouldn't want to make less than that."

Leon hired me and I started the following Monday. The feed store was far from perfect for me. It felt strange to be working there, coming from a retail store and a position where I had my own staff, where I could use my creativity to build and maintain a steady business, a place where I felt proud of my work and accomplishments. Working at an animal feed store felt like a step backward. Selling pig feed didn't exactly require a lot of creativity, nor was there a lot of variety to the work. But I knew I was fortunate to be there, to have a job. And there was very little pressure. I liked Leon and Ann who both made me feel like family. And most of the customers were loyal and friendly. I was happy to be back at work. I felt in control again.

Around the premises of the feed store I noticed cats. Lots of them. Maybe thirty to forty. Feral cats, I would learn. Pretty much a nuisance is how they were described. But I soon began to feed them, waiting until the store would close for the day and the customers had left. I felt sorry for the cats. Some of them seemed healthy enough, others were in obvious need of veterinary treatment. The help would leave some food for them but never enough. Mostly the cats had to hunt for their food. Most kept a wary distance, although a few were friendly and I imagined must have been pets at one time but had since been abandoned. The task of taking care of the cats was overwhelming but I began feeling responsible for them.

At home, it was the dogs that kept me busy. The puppies continued to grow. Sheba had adjusted to her blindness as well as to her daily insulin shots and several weekly visits to the vet to make sure her diabetes remained under control. She didn't run with the puppies anymore but she still fussed over them, especially Little Evita. The two seemed to have a special bond. Evita learned how to let Sheba know when she was approaching her, somehow aware that her mother was unable to see. She'd crawl slowly and deliberately over to Sheba, making little noises with her mouth. Often they'd fall asleep side by side, Evita nestled into Sheba's tummy.

Little Evita was a tall girl with a beautiful body. Both Mika and Evita were well-built and both were show quality. Some of the others people who showed Afghan hounds didn't want Evita or Mika in the show rings. They didn't want Canio in the show ring, either. This I discovered one day while looking for a professional handler to show Canio. A woman handler told me that the other owners didn't want to see Canio's breeder Marvin Johnson get any credit for the victories of one of his dogs. Show dog business was a tough, competitive sport. But I was there for the pleasure of working and showing my dogs. I loved doing it and had no intention of being in the breeding business.

If there was a bond between Sheba and Evita, there was a bond between them all. They were a family. And as happens in any family, there was tragedy. Mika was less than two years old when she became ill and was diagnosed with lymphosarcoma, a rare and rapidly fatal form of leukemia. We treated her with chemotherapy but when it became apparent that she was in severe pain, I made the decision to let her go. At the vet's office, on a quiet September morning in 1988, she died in my arms. She was just twenty-one months old.

The death of Mika struck me with an intense sadness. James felt it too and we both wrote poems in remembrance of Mika to try to somehow work through our grief. But we were not alone in our sadness. The little girl felt it, too.

I had not been able to help the little girl, or find help for her. I blamed myself. I was angry at myself. I could not adequately explain to anyone what was going on with me. I felt as though people stopped listening the moment I started to speak. The frustration was overwhelming. I knew, and the little girl knew, that not one person in the whole goddamned world cared. No one understood. The sadness of Mika's death seemed to send us both to the edge.

The morning after Mika died, I was startled to hear a voice say, *You promised me. You promised me.* I had no idea what it meant. What was promised? To whom?

And then there was beating on the pillows on the bed. Someone was angry, though it sounded more like frustration than rage. And then she repeated it: *You promised me. You promised me.* Then more beating on the pillows.

I knew it was me talking, but it was involuntary. I was grieving Mika, my Little Sparrow. And I realized that the little girl was grieving, too. So was the protector. "*Oh God, help me!* she cried, and with her hand covering her mouth, she let out a long, silent scream. Then she collapsed on the bed.

She lay there, arms crossed over her body as if hugging herself, as if to protect her body from harm. Tears rolled down the side of her face onto the pillow and my heart ached for her. Part of me wanted to turn my back on her but I knew I needed to stay. The tears rolling down my face wetting my cheeks interrupted the thoughts and brought me back to reality and I quickly rose from the bed and sat in a chair. I looked at the clock and knew I had to get ready for work. There was no time for tears and I took control again. It was the first and only time that I felt one of the girls take over this way. Though it surprised me, it did not frighten me. If it were to happen again, I knew I could get control back. Later I would wonder if it was the seven-year-old or the twelve-year-old. And I would wonder at the promise she had referenced. I would never know what it was, although I often thought it had something to do with Brookwood—the things I had said in group therapy that I did not hear myself say.

Back at the feed store I continued working with the cats, taking care of them as best I could. I had grown especially fond of a particular tabby. For the longest time I had seen her studying me at a distance, not quite sure what to make of me. I spoke to her often and I could tell she wanted to get closer but was afraid to. Finally, one day I walked very slowly towards her. She remained in place as I reached out and touched her. She was trembling slightly but I could not miss the very soft purring underneath her thick coat of fur.

In a second the encounter was over. The little tabby darted off, stopping at a safe distance and looking back toward me, watching as I poured the fresh food and water into the bowls. I talked to her and she meowed softly, her feet kneading the ground as though it were a wool blanket instead of the sandy soil. She was still close enough that I could hear her purring very quietly.

My task done for the day, I slowly backed away, thinking that I was getting very close to making friends with the little tabby. A couple more days and I might be able to hold her, perhaps.

The following Monday I drove into the yard and was startled by what I saw, startled by what was missing. Not a single cat was in sight. The grounds were deserted. The food I had left on Friday had hardly been touched. I filled the bowl again that night but the food was all still there on Tuesday morning. The cats had gone. Even an old friendly black and white cat that everyone petted and talked to was gone. I wondered what could possibly have possessed all the cats to hide so suddenly. I asked around and finally in a hushed voice someone said the cats had been shot over the weekend. "Population control," he added. That thought had crossed my mind but I did not want to believe it. Further questions were met with a shrug.

On Wednesday morning I noticed blood on the side of the water bowl. A wounded cat was out there, somewhere. I walked around to the large storage building across from the office but saw nothing unusual.

I did my best to go about my work, but the office was tense and felt suddenly different to me—cold and unfamiliar. Often during the day I became distracted with thoughts of the missing cats. The thought of the little tabby kept coming to my mind and tears frequently blurred my eyes. Where could she be?

Then late in the afternoon I heard a weak meow coming from right outside the door. I rushed outside to see her by the food bowl—the little tabby. She was trying to eat and as I got closer she looked up at me and let out another weak meow. Then I saw her face. Part of her mouth had been blown away. The little tabby was barely alive. I grabbed a towel from the office and I wrapped her with it; she did not fight or move away from me then. Her little body was cold and had the smell of decaying flesh.

Without a word to anyone I left the premises and I drove to the veterinarian. I had been trying to cultivate in the little tabby a trust for humans and she had just been beginning to trust me. I wondered at the type of people who could shoot such innocent animals. And I wondered if there were other innocents out there—wounded, cold, and dying alone.

I held the little tabby in my arms while the veterinarian put her to sleep, just as I had held my little Mika just a few months before. I spoke tenderly to her and underneath her fur I could feel her softly purring until her heart came to a stop. And then the little tabby was gone.

CHAPTER FOURTEEN

Evita

~

FOR SEVERAL DAYS I COULD NOT RETURN TO THE FEED store. I went into a kind of shock. The deaths of the cats, and especially the death of the tabby, coming on the heels of Mika's death, were almost more than I could handle. But I soon found my anguish turning to anger. I wanted justice for the feral cats. I wanted justice for the little tabby. I went to the Sonoma County Humane Society and I went to Sonoma County Animal Control. Neither was of any help.

Meanwhile, the bookkeeper from Barlas was calling me every day; Leon wanted to talk to me. Finally I went into the store and closed the door of Leon's office behind me and we talked. Yes, it was Leon's property, but Leon had not killed the cats. In time, I would learn it was another employee, a young man, still in high school. It was technically illegal to shoot the cats, but it was a law rarely enforced in rural Sonoma County. Killing cats was simply what some farmers did. It was acceptable. The cats had virtually no protection, no chance. But that day Leon and I struck a deal in his office. I would continue to work there, but there would be no more killing. And with Leon providing cat food at cost, I would take care of the cats.

Cats eventually began to populate the grounds of the feed store again, often coming in on large, double-trailer loads of hay. Leon made it clear to the other employees that no harm was to come to any of them. Often, mostly in the spring, little kittens came in too—some just days old, no bigger than mice, orphaned from their mothers. I began taking them home with me and keeping them there until they were weaned, typically somewhere around eight weeks. Then I'd find homes for them. I designed fliers and posted them all around town—at veterinary clinics, other feed stores, wherever I found a bulletin board that accepted fliers. I ran newspaper ads in Sonoma County, Marin County, and even in the San Francisco newspapers. I struck a deal with the Marin Humane Society and they agreed to place the kittens for which I could not find homes in their adoption program.

The adult cats could not, for the most part, be tamed. They could not be found homes. But I came across Forgotten Felines of Sonoma County, a recently formed organization dedicated to feral cats. They taught me to trap the adult cats and bring them to the vet to be spayed or neutered, procedures that Forgotten Felines paid for from contributions. Then I'd return the cats and make certain they were fed daily. Later I would do volunteer work for

Forgotten Felines, to repay them for their help.

With the kittens and my job at the feed store, I was working long hours. I cleaned the cats, bottle fed the kittens, and took care of all of them. The youngest kittens had to be fed every four hours, day and night. I'd bring them to work with me and bottle-feed them as I waited on customers. I'd trap the adult cats after work during times when I had no kittens to feed. The kittens, especially, were little miracles to me. It struck me that I was essentially their replacement mother and that I was helping to provide for them the gift of life.

Once I brought a litter of kittens home and finding no homes for three of them, I eventually took the three to the Marin Humane Society. James was furious. Not for bringing the kittens home, but for taking them away. James had become attached to them. He drove to the Humane Society, but they knew who he was and refused to release the kittens back to him. We had an agreement, after all. And the Society's goal, and mine, was for the kittens to be found homes—not a single home for the mass of them. Left to his own devices, James would have allowed fifty kittens or more to reside with us. James left the Humane Society but then returned, hurt and angry and argumentative. "I'm sorry," he was again told, "but we can't release them to you." Then James sent a friend, but the staff at the Society saw through the attempt and refused the friend as well.

Working with the kittens, though exhausting at times, was therapy for me, healing for the soul. But not just for me. Trapping the cats was often very difficult. Feral cats are wild cats, distrusting and fearful. More than once, in the actions of the cats, I saw myself back in Jim Fraser's office on the day he had tried to teach me self-defense techniques. He had made me lie down and had knelt beside me and I had rolled away from him and had run, panic-stricken into a corner where I had crouched, frantic and frightened. It was the little girl in the corner that day. She was as a feral cat. It was impossible not to see it, and I began to understand why I had come to connect with the cats so strongly. I knew how they felt and I felt sorry for them. And just as the dogs helped tame the twelve-year-old, the feral cats seemed to help lessen the fears of the seven-year-old. One night, as I was falling asleep, I heard someone say, "He choked me...and I did not die." Perhaps it was the seven-year-old. But as the cats began to trust me, as their fears and misgivings ever so slowly abated, so did the fears and misgivings of the little girl. So too did her sadness. My "kitten therapy", as I came to refer to it, was infinitely more helpful than any therapy I had received from the psychiatric profession.

~

IN THE SAN FRANCISCO EXAMINER ONE DAY, I read an article about a conference being held for psychiatrists specifically on dissociative disorders. Leading the conference was a Dr. David Spiegel, associate professor of psychiatry at Stanford University Medical Center. I wrote to him. I didn't want to let him know I was suffering from a dissociative disorder, but I wanted to make it clear to him that the disorder existed.

I could understand the skepticism within the profession; there were too many sensationalistic accounts. But competent and dedicated professionals should be able to differentiate between the real and the manufactured. "Much more interest should be placed on treatment," I wrote, "rather than trying to decide if such phenomena actually exist." And I added that the worst thing mental health professionals could do was prescribe mind-altering drugs that disrupt the tightly controlled mind of a person suffering from multiple personality disorder.

I wrote the letter to vent. I hadn't expected a reply but within a few days I received one. Speigel kindly thanked me for my thoughts. And having apparently read between the lines, he passed along the name of a psychiatrist as well. The referral happened to be the person who was in charge of mental health for all of Sonoma County. By then I had been to mental health experts who were considered some of the best in Northern California. I had lost my faith in the profession. I feared it, actually, ever since the forced hospitalization at Ross Valley. I didn't follow up with the name Speigel had given me. I was doing fine with my dogs and my kitten therapy. What I really wanted to do was to educate others.

As for the dogs, on a day soon after Mika's passing, I had a premonition while looking at her picture above the desk on the family room wall. I walked by the photograph and looked into her eyes, just as I would do every day. On that day, a feeling of dread came over me. I turned to look at Evita who was resting on the floor and I felt a sudden sense that she, too, was not long for this earth. The thought of lymphosarcoma came into my mind and I found myself crying while hugging my Little Evita. She was beautiful, and she reminded me of the little girl because she was fearful of people until she got to know them. If someone came over to visit, Evita would scrunch up in the farthest corner of the sofa, trying to make herself small. Or she'd hide behind James or me.

Within just a few months, Little Evita began to show signs of discomfort. She was not eating well, had diarrhea, and was losing weight. The veterinarian found the symptoms suspicious and sent me to the specialty clinic where Mika had been treated before she died. At the clinic, Dr. Magne saw Evita and I explained her symptoms, symptoms very much like Mika's. Dr. Magne assured me that I was overreacting. "It would be an extremely rare coincidence," he said. "Lymphosarcoma is rare enough for one dog, let alone two. I'm sure she'll be fine." He prescribed some medication and then convinced me that a bone marrow test would be unnecessary. It was welcome news.

A few weeks passed and Evita was not improving. I returned and this time insisted on the bone marrow test. Magne seemed annoyed at the request and although he performed the test, in his certitude that nothing was wrong, he elected not to send the specimen to the lab on that day, a fact I would learn when I called to get the test results. At that point, I made an appointment for Evita at the University of California in Davis where my fears were confirmed. By then, Evita was in the advanced stages of lymphosarcoma.

I was too sad to be angry at Magne. I only wanted to

make life as easy as possible for Little Evita. I did everything I could to keep her comfortable and to make her life as painless as I could. I gave her love and affection and spent more time with her. But the cancer progressed quickly. When I felt the time had come to let her go, James resisted the idea. He had grown very attached to all the dogs. "She's in pain; she will not survive this, James," I said. "She's dying and I don't want her to suffer." It was obvious. Her breathing was labored. Her gums were pale. She didn't meet me at the door anymore. She'd lift her head from the floor and wag her tail to let me know she heard me, but she was too tired to get up. Finally, I convinced James and he accompanied me to the clinic.

Once there, however, the veterinarian had other ideas. Though I explained that Evie had cancer, was terminal, and in pain, he challenged my decision. "I don't know what they've found at Davis or how they're treating her," he told me, "but I'm not seeing anything that warrants putting her down." It was all James needed to hear. I was alone in the decision to end Little Evita's life and I began to have second thoughts. I felt like a monster. Against my better judgment, we took Evita home.

It was just a few weeks before Christmas, 1989, and I felt nothing of the season. I had grandchildren by then and there were plans for the holiday, but I didn't want to have Christmas that year. I didn't want to shop for gifts for the kids or grandkids. I didn't want to cook, I didn't even want to smile. But I went about my life, went to work, went shopping, kept taking care of the feral cats.

Meanwhile, Little Evita was dying. On the evening of December 13, I went Christmas shopping after work. Truthfully, I didn't want to go home. It was painful to watch my Little Evie die. When I did return home I made a bed beside her and I lay next to her for hours. I talked to her and sang to her. I finally went to bed when I heard James's alarm clock. Just after dozing off, I heard James call my name. "Little Evita died," he said. It was about 5:30 a.m. When I walked into the family room, there she was, lying between her mother and father, cuddled against Sheba. Canio raised his head, looked up at me, and laid his head back down again. Sheba didn't move.

In just a little more than a year's time, I had lost the two puppies I had bred almost exclusively for the purpose of helping the girls, gifts to them of a sort. It had never been coincidence, in my mind, that Sheba had only had a litter of two. And it didn't seem like coincidence that both puppies had died of the exact same rare disease. I had had Mika and Evita brought into the world for my own discrete purposes and I consequently felt responsible for their deaths. Along with my heartache, I felt guilt. I felt regret, too, at having been talked out of putting Evita to sleep. I knew she'd spent her last days in pain. And yet I knew of the effect the lives of the puppies, however short, had on the girls. How instrumental they had been in the healing process. In a sense, the puppies had given their lives for the girls. In a sense, they had given their lives for me.

CHAPTER FIFTEEN
Therapist

∼

THAT SAME MORNING, JAMES AND I DROVE EVITA'S body back to U.C. Davis. I wanted a record of the cause of her death. I could not forget the condescending attitude of the local veterinarian, dismissing the possibility of cancer and then, when I had insisted on the bone marrow test, failing to send it to the lab. "She'll be fine," he had said. The necropsy report was three single-spaced pages, a damning list of symptoms and abnormalities that no veterinarian should have been able to miss. Little Evita's body was full of cancer. The report ended with a summary comment: "Extensive thrombosis seen in the lung and the heart... a paraneoplastic syndrome seen in various types of cancer...related to necrotic tumor cells...*compatible with a lymphosarcoma.*"

The death of my Little Evita was difficult for me on several levels. In addition to the guilt and regret, there was, of course, the normal grief, but there was also anger at the veterinarian and I couldn't help but note the parallels of my experiences with the two different professions—veterinary science and psychiatry. We'd been a victim of both, the girls and I.

I threw myself into work and continued to focus on my feral cat project. I needed to work and I needed routine. I also started becoming more interested in politics and activism, an interest I first discovered after my J.C. Penney experience, losing my job and finding myself with no recourse and no means by which to dispute the actions of Stuart and the company. Too, I wanted to give voice to the feral cats of Sonoma County, who could be indiscriminately shot without repercussion. Add in the indifference shown me from two different disciplines of medicine, and there was no shortage of targets. The world was full of injustice, it seemed to me, and I remembered a quote from Bobby Kennedy: "…when we fail to speak up and speak out, we strike a blow against freedom and decency and justice."

I needed to learn how to speak up and speak out, and I joined the Sonoma County National Organization for Women. In February of 1991, I organized a Sonoma County NOW workshop on sexual harassment in the workplace and introduced the speakers. One was an attorney who spoke about sexual harassment law. We became friends and later that year I stopped by his office and we talked about my J.C Penney experience and then I found myself opening up more to him, telling him about my dissociative disorder, though not everything, of course. "I read a recent magazine article about multiple personality disorder," he said, and he dug out an issue of a local Sonoma magazine. "Here, you can keep it."

"Secret Voices," was a case study of a patient of a Sebastopol psychologist named Trula LaCalle. The article was based on LaCalle's book *Voices*. I read the article; later I would read the book and it would impress me as being a bit phony, much like *The Three Faces of Eve* had seemed to me. It seemed sensationalistic. In *Voices*, as with *Eve* and as with the famous story of *Sybil* that followed, the patient spoke through his personalities. He became them; he acted as them. This had not been my experience. Dissociative disorder was real enough, it seemed to me, without adding melodrama. *Sybil*, in particular, had become especially controversial, with accusations that the patient's disorder had been encouraged by her doctor and her story essentially fabricated. The whole idea of repressed memories—and it was repressed memories, of course, that had triggered my dissociative tendencies—had come under attack in the 1980s with a prominent case about a daycare center in which overzealous therapists planted ideas in the heads of children about abuse suffered at the hands of the daycare workers. The implanted ideas even included memories of satanic rituals. None of it had really happened.

And so I chafed at the theatrics, thinking they were at least partially responsible for the seeming lack of credibility for the disorders. The hyperbole, it seemed to me, was one reason I had been strapped to a bed at Ross Valley and forced to take medication. It was why the doctor there had asked me about my repressed memories and had then said simply, "It's not true, is it?"

At that time, however, I had only read LaCalle's article, not her book, and she seemed like someone who knew her business, who knew about the disorders that had been plaguing me and who knew, at the least, that the disorders were real. Yes, I had lost faith in the psychiatric profession, but surely Dr. LaCalle could restore it. She could help me. Sebastopol was only a half-hour drive away.

In October 1991, I went to see Dr. LaCalle, a petite woman in her fifties, slim and well-dressed. She came across as confident and self-assured. I told her about my repressed memories, and I told her about the little girl and how I wanted to get in touch with her. I told her that I did not want long term therapy, maybe just five or six sessions. I told her about my stay at Brookwood and gave her permission to acquire my records. I mentioned that I had said something there that I had not heard and that it had apparently been something of some significance, based on how I'd been treated afterwards.

The appointments went well. After the second one, Dr. LaCalle recommended hypnosis for five or six sessions, beginning with the next one. I felt comfortable with her and I looked forward to our next appointment. I became excited, thinking that I might be able to learn more about the little girl. And perhaps, too, learn what I had said at Brookwood.

When I arrived for the next appointment, something felt immediately different. The receptionist, friendly towards me my first couple visits, barely acknowledged me. After a few minutes of waiting, Dr. LaCalle came out and asked me into her office. She sat down at her desk and crossed her arms and stared at me with a cold look on her face. I noticed a tripod with a camera in the corner of the room and I assumed that maybe she was planning to videotape the session. But something was wrong. She continued to glare at me and say nothing. I broke the silence. "I've been looking forward to this session," I offered.

"So, what is it that you want?" LaCalle asked in a cold and sarcastic tone. Both the question and the tone took me aback.

"Well, we were going to do hypnosis," I said at last.

"Okay. So how do you want to do this?"

I didn't know how to reply. Eventually she began to put me into trance, but I was uneasy and it was difficult. Still, I desperately wanted to reach the little girl and I forced myself to concentrate and at one point I felt the little girl and extended my hand to her but she disappeared. "I'm sorry," I said. "I cannot continue. Something seems wrong." Soon, tears were running down my face.

"This is my last session with you," LaCalle said at that point, "I won't see you anymore."

"But...why?"

"I'm afraid I'm going to have to terminate our treatment," she said, as if the statement was an explanation.

"But I don't understand. Why? Can you refer me elsewhere at least?"

"I'm afraid not. Marcelle, you should know that I'm the top expert in this field. When it comes to multiple personality disorder, other psychiatrists and psychologists and therapists from all over come to me. They consult with *me*. I give lectures on the subject. I presented a lecture just two day ago, as a matter of fact."

I left her office in a daze. I sat in my car several minutes trying to sort out what had just happened. Eventually it occurred to me that her recounting of her qualifications seemed calculated to answer skepticism, skepticism which I did not possess. And I suddenly wondered what Brookwood had shared with her after I had given her permission to get my records from them. What had I said? I remembered voicing my distrust of the psychiatric profession. "Someday I'll tell others all about it," I remembered saying. And I remembered the attitude from the staff afterwards. "I think this one's only here to inspect the facility," one of the nurses had said. Too, I had voiced my concerns to Dr. LaCalle about the profession during our very first session. It had been, in fact, why she had agreed to five or six sessions, and not a longer-term strategy. But we had stopped in the middle of just the third.

I wrote to LaCalle the next day, asking what happened. Why had I been given such a cold reception by her and why had she terminated her treatment? She wrote back, claiming my goals for the therapy had been "successfully fulfilled." This, though I had left her office in tears. I next sent a letter threatening legal action and she wrote a five-page letter in reply that seemed calculated to cover her actions. During that third session, I had apparently "implied that (I) could do things better on (my) own." She had "assumed" that that was how I would prefer to proceed. Her sudden and insensitive dismissal of me? We simply had "differing perceptions" of that.

To me, it seemed as though she had come to realize, against her original instincts, that my problems were real, that I was sincere in my desire for treatment, that no matter what she might have read into my initial comments about the psychiatric profession, or what she might have been told by the staff at Brookwood, I was a patient who needed help. But by then it was too late. All she could do was try to justify her decision to send me away.

Eventually I filed a complaint with the State of California Board of Behavioral Science Examiners. Abandoning a client is a punishable offense. LaCalle had terminated my treatment without forewarning or referrals. Theoretically, at least, she had placed my life in danger. The Board wrote back: "We have reviewed the information you submitted. We could not clearly and convincingly conclude a violation under the issues of abandonment. Thank you for contacting the Board. We regret we could not be of more assistance to you."

I filed a lawsuit in small claims court. The judge said the case was too complicated for small claims and sent us to superior court. There, the judge listened as I recounted how LaCalle had dropped me. Then he turned to LaCalle who said, "This is all news to me. She only wanted to have a couple sessions and that's what she got. She didn't have insurance for any further sessions." It was a lie. I had insurance and I told the judge. But there was nothing more, really, to say. It was a professional psychiatrist's word against the word of a psychiatric patient. I didn't stand a chance. I told LaCalle as much in the hallway, afterwards, after the judge had ruled in her favor. "Of course he was going to believe you," I said. She turned to me and smiled, not saying a word.

Trula LaCalle was the last mental health expert whose help I would ever venture to seek.

~

THE COMPANY OF THE DOGS, meanwhile, continued to be therapeutic for me. Sheba went for her daily walks holding her head up high, like the proud Afghan she was, her blindness doing nothing to impair her spirit. Canio continued to look out for her around the house, promptly warning her about the cat or occasional critter that might make it into the backyard. The two were like an old married couple who had been together so long that they no longer needed words to communicate. I regulated Sheba's diabetes very well on my own. She was on a strict diet and did well for several years.

But then in January of 1992, Sheba suddenly stopped eating. I agonized over what to do. I hesitated taking her to U.C. Davis. I wanted to keep her close to home so that I could visit with her as often as possible. She needed me and I felt it was better for her if I could be with her. And I was reluctant to take her to the local vets, given my experiences with them.

Finally, I decided to take her to a small clinic close to

home where she had been seen before. "She needs hospital-ization," Dr. Howse said to me after he examined her. "We're closing for the three day M.L.K. weekend and she'll have to be transferred to the Sonoma County Emergency Veterinary Clinic for the weekend."

I hesitated. How could I explain my relationship with the emergency clinic and the chief of staff? Just the thought was beginning to make my eyes well up. Little Evita's painful death had been more than two years prior, but I couldn't speak about it yet.

"I had a serious disagreement there with Michael Magne," I finally told Dr. Howse. I explained the misdiag-nosis.

"Listen," Dr. Howse said, "Sheba is very ill. She needs to be hospitalized with constant supervision. The Emer-gency Veterinary Clinic is the best place for her and I assure you, she will receive all the care she needs there. Trust me," he added.

He was probably right, I reasoned, and I allowed Sheba to be transferred. And I felt relieved and reassured when Dr. Croley from the Sonoma County Emergency Veterinary Clinic called me several times on Friday evening and even during the night to give me updates on Sheba's condition.

But on Saturday morning when I went in to visit her, I was sent not to where Sheba was, but to an office. I thought Sheba must have died. It was the office of a Dr. LaMar and after introducing herself to me, she began to speak quietly and cautiously. "This is not something that I would do myself," she said. "I want you to understand that. Dr. Magne is the chief of staff here and when he came in this morning and saw Sheba he ordered that she be removed from the clinic. Please understand, this is not something I would recommend. But I have no choice. Dr. Magne is in charge here and without his approval, we cannot treat Sheba."

The words didn't quite register in my mind. "You mean I have to take Sheba home? Right now? She is very ill. Dr. Howse was very clear about it. Where would I take her on a Saturday? She won't survive the weekend." I tried to keep calm but my hands were shaking.

I turned toward the patients' room and Dr. LaMar followed me to Sheba's crate. When Sheba heard me she lifted her head and tried to stand up but she was too weak. I heard Dr. LaMar behind me whisper, "Oh, God!" and I realized she had not been made aware of Sheba's condition. I turned to her and asked for the medical records. She handed the records over along with an invoice and I carried Sheba out to my car.

The Chief of Staff, Michael Magne, the vet who misdiagnosed Little Evita, had ordered Sheba out. I had apparently bruised his ego by taking Little Evita to Davis and daring to question his diagnosis. Now he was getting even.

I laid Sheba down on the back seat and I stayed with her for several minutes, holding a hand to my mouth to keep the screams from escaping. I couldn't think rationally. Sheba was dying a slow death and I felt as though I wanted to curl up against her and die with her.

Eventually I started the car and began the drive home. I searched my soul during the fifteen-minute drive, wondering if this was somehow my fault. But I knew that what had been allowed to happen was very wrong. People need to know about this, I thought. "When we fail to speak up and speak out," the man had said before his death. Yes, people needed to know.

I laid Sheba down on her bed in the kitchen by the sliding door and I sat with her for a while as I tried to calm down and control my anger. I spoke to Sheba gently, and I apologized for human behavior. I swore to her, as I had sworn to Little Evita, that her suffering would not be in vain. Then I called the Veterinary Medical Teaching Hospital, University of California, Davis, and explained Sheba's condition. They said to bring her in after 3:00 p.m. "By then we'll have a specialist on duty," the operator said.

My next call was to the *Press Democrat.* I asked to speak to Jim Sweeney, the same writer I had contacted before about veterinary malpractice. I told him about Sheba being thrown out of the emergency clinic and again I asked him to consider doing a story. "I cannot do this alone," I told him. "What will it take before anyone helps?" As before, Sweeney was reluctant. I hung up feeling alone and helpless. I knew I'd been too emotional talking to Sweeney. I could hardly speak. But wouldn't a good journalist want to pick up on the story? I knew how badly Sheba had been treated. And I wondered how others might be treated, too. Other pet owners who might not be natives, who might speak with an accent. Sweeney could have made a difference, not only for Sheba but for other animals, too. I knew my dogs weren't the only ones with stories.

After seeing that Sheba was comfortable I went upstairs and took a long shower to gather my thoughts and to wash the smell of the clinic from my body. I needed to do something. It was clear that help would come from no one. I was alone and I needed to do something to release the pain and anger in my heart. And soon the activist in me began to plan.

When I came downstairs, James was home and he wanted to know about Sheba. I collected myself as best I could and told him what had happened. "The Rohnert Park clinic threw her out of the hospital. We need to take her to Davis." He didn't ask why. He knew the reason and I saw the hurt in his eyes. James, of course, always had difficulty showing his feelings but I knew he was hurting and probably felt helpless. He had played a large role in Sheba's life. He walked her and Canio every day after work and he had been the one to feed them if I had to work late or attend meetings.

The ride to Davis was quiet and when we arrived at the hospital they had a stretcher ready and two helpers came out to take Sheba out of the car and onto the stretcher. Sheba didn't move. She let everyone handle her without any reaction. But then, that was the way Sheba was; she was used to being handled by doctors and helpers. She was a gentle and sweet dog. But at times, she could also show that she had a mind of her own. If she didn't want to do something, she'd let you know by stamping her front feet on the ground and letting out a deep hound *woof,* with a few growls to let you know she meant business. Then I would say, "Sheba, want to go with me?"and that would do it. She'd stand up with her neck stretched out, wanting to know where we were going.

At Davis, Sheba would be in the intensive care unit for several days in critical condition. Then it would be several more days out of ICU to recuperate. She was stabilized with a new brand of insulin that would keep her metabolism under control. Sheba would survive.

The day after Sheba was hospitalized in Davis, it was cold and rainy and blustery. But I had my material ready to begin to speak for Sheba: a picket sign and flyers to pass out, to tell people what had happened at the clinic. I was nervous to be out there all by myself, but determined to do it. I had contacted the police department about the laws on public protest and I knew my rights and I made sure that I could prove everything I had written in the flyers. For two hours I walked the busy street holding my sign. *Critically ill, blind dog thrown out of this clinic.*

Because of the weather, there weren't many people on the street but as cars passed and slowed down to read the sign I received many thumbs-up and people would blow their horns. Two workers from the clinic came out to see what was going on. I wanted an apology, I explained. And my money back. For Sheba and for my Little Evita. They walked back inside.

Afterwards, I wrote a letter to the Humane Society of Sonoma County and asked for an investigation into the emergency clinic in Rohnert Park. They would not investigate. Executive director Dan Knapp wrote back, saying there were no grounds for the Humane Society to perform an investigation. The reply puzzled me, but I was not deterred.

Doing some research, I discovered that the Sonoma

County Emergency Veterinary Clinic was owned by two veterinarians: Fred Groverman and David McCrystle. Neither actually worked at the clinic. Groverman had another veterinary clinic for farm animals in Cotati, a nearby town. He was also on the board of directors of the Petaluma Valley Hospital. He was well-known and respected in the community. McCrystle worked at his clinic in Healdsburg, where he resided. And he happened to be the president of the board of directors of the Humane Society of Sonoma County. The editorial director for the *Press Democrat* was also on the board of director of the Humane Society of Sonoma County. As was the mayor of Santa Rosa. And then I realized why I'd been unable to generate any interest from Jim Sweeney in doing an expose and why Dan Knapp did not want to do an investigation. The clinic, the Humane Society, and the *Press Democrat* were all connected.

In the meantime I prepared to file a lawsuit against the Rohnert Park facility. Dr. Groverman, DVM, came to my home to discuss the situation, trying to discourage me from filing the suit, saying I was too "emotional" to go to court. I later responded in a letter: "You must ask yourself if $844.24 reimbursement to settle this dispute is worth the scandal and embarrassment to the veterinary profession a lawsuit would undoubtedly create." A few weeks later, I received two checks from their insurance company. One for Little Evita for $416.50, and the other for Sheba for $427.74.

No one ever apologized.

Sheba lived comfortably for more than a year afterwards. Eventually, however, it was her time. She was tired.

She died in my arms, peacefully, while I thought how gentle she had been and how much she had given, without any expectation. And I thought how Sheba had been not only my dog, she had been my therapist. Time and again, she stood in for the best that any human could offer. She saw me through the worst times of my life. All the dogs had.

I thought of all this and more, holding Sheba close to me in the clinic on the day she died. She was lying on her favorite blanket. And as she slipped away, she seemed at peace, as though she were asleep. She looked perfectly natural, save for the tears that were dropping and settling on her soft fur.

Sheba

CHAPTER SIXTEEN

Forgiveness

~

IN NOVEMBER OF 1992, MY MOTHER DIED. SHE WAS eighty-five. I had a chance to say goodbye to her as a nurse at her hospital put a phone to her ear. I was the last to speak to her. Shortly afterwards, she passed away. Though we had frequently talked by phone over the years, the last time I had actually seen my mother was in September of 1984. We'd had exactly one phone conversation about the events that I had repressed. I don't believe she ever told anyone else what she'd told me.

I didn't go to the funeral. Death was always more than I could handle. The last funeral I had attended was in 1953, when I was eighteen. My Grandmother Brault had passed away in a hospice in Sherbrooke where I was then living. Before she died we were all gathered around her bedside and I had been overcome by the sheer somberness of the situation and had fainted and had to be carried from the room.

I waited in the hallway for her death to come about. At the funeral, I remember how distraught my mother was, sobbing uncontrollably as the casket was being lowered into the ground.

I struggled with confused feelings after my mother died. I knew her life had not been easy. I thought about my father and about the beatings and how we girls had been sent to the boarding school. And of course there was my father's death, at the hands of one of her sons. And I wondered what else happened in my mother's life that I didn't know about, that I would never know about. Her life with my father and with twelve children could not have been an easy one. And yet…I could not forget her words to me on the phone that day: *Your father told me he was sorry, Marcelle. It's okay. Your father was very sorry.*

Maybe what I wanted was an apology from my mother. For her enabling my father, for not stepping in somehow. Maybe what I wanted was for somebody to take responsibility. Nobody ever had. The incident was forgotten, and not just by me. And I couldn't help but think that the silence from everyone involved went hand in hand with my own denial and repression. But the little girl, of course—she could never forget. And it struck me that when a child dies, there's never a shortage of grief and regret and second-guessing. There is none of this for a survivor.

I continued with my feral cat project and I continued to be involved with Sonoma County NOW. The feral cat project was healing. NOW was empowering. I served on the board of NOW as action coordinator and became a member of the Democratic Central Committee as alternate for assembly woman Vivien Brownshvag. I was even invited to the Clinton inauguration. I didn't attend. Through the years, no matter the progress I had made with my emotional well-being, I had never lost certain fears. I could not be in an airplane, for instance, where I'd be enclosed and where I didn't have control over my environment. Not wanting to drive to Washington, D.C., I chose to stay home. I was still afraid of the dark, as well, and it caused me to eventually resign from the committee. The meetings were always at night and I was afraid to walk to my car alone. You cannot tell people you are afraid of the dark and be a member of the committee.

In 1995, Canio died, peacefully, on the very sofa that he had claimed as his years prior when he had tricked me into getting up to go to the door to let him out. And I reflected once again on the therapeutic help the four Afghan hounds had provided me and the girls. That same year, a professor with a doctorate in psychology from Stanford, wrote a book called *The Intelligence of Dogs*. Dr. Stanley Coren ranked the Afghan hound as dead last in degree of working intelligence. I found it amusing. Essentially, in the course of my self-treatment, I had replaced his entire profession with the Afghan hound.

James and I had the animals in common, but virtually nothing else. He retired in 1997 and did nothing but sit around the house. We had nothing to say to each other. The house was big and there were just the two of us and things were awkward and cold. I filed for divorce. James fought it bitterly. He had no love for me, but he had no desire to split our assets. I think he would have preferred to see me homeless or living in my car.

We went to court and he testified that the marriage had essentially ended the day I had decided to take another bedroom. I had withheld sex, he said. We weren't husband and wife by any definition. When it was my turn, I told the judge that I had been a faithful wife and by all outside appearances, we were indeed husband and wife. The judge sided with me. James bought me out of the house and I left.

I took my sons' last name—Aldéma's last name, thinking my maiden name of Drouin was too foreign, too difficult to pronounce. And while I was at it, I changed my middle name, too. It had been Luce, but I legally changed it to Evie. I always liked the name. It was what I had frequently called Little Evita, having shortened her name when talking to her or calling her to simply "E.V". Because Little Evita reminded me of the little girl—just as the feral cats had, shy and aloof around other people, yet gentle and sweet—I decided to name the little girl Evie.

The idea of giving the little girl a name was a way, I thought, to give her some much-needed affirmation. She could know she was loved and cared for. She was somebody again—not a nameless, lost soul who had suffered a horrifying ordeal and then had been forgotten. It helped. Over time, I could finally separate the little girl from the terrible secret she had kept hidden for so many years. I would never be able to fully accept what had happened in the basement of our house in Lac-Mégantic. To do so would mean reliving it. But I could not ignore the little girl. She was a part of me. And so my new name included the little girl within me: Marcelle Evie Guy.

In September of 2003, I traveled to Lac-Mégantic. I had not been back since I had visited in 1973, before moving to California. It had been thirty years, but I sensed that I had to return. I knew I would never be whole until I went back. I drove from Petaluma to Maine (I would not fly, of course) and then crossed the border into Canada. My siblings all knew I was coming. Six brothers and five sisters—some of whom still lived there, others who were scattered about in Montréal or Quebec—all made plans to see me. I would be there for a two-week visit.

But my very first stop was the reason I had returned to the town of my lost childhood. I pulled into the cemetery and approached a worker. "Can you tell me where I might find the grave of Wellie Drouin?" Soon I was standing in front of my father's grave, my mother's grave right next to it. I said a prayer and then told them both that I forgave them. I told my mother that I understood. I could blame her no longer. I felt sorry for her. Hers was a life of sacrifices for her family.

My father remained an enigma to me. Impossibly, I still loved my father. For a time, I had felt responsible for his death. I remembered the fire at Inspector Breton's house, very shortly after I had been sent there for tutoring as a child and I had not liked it there. I remembered the time I had been raped in Montréal and that the man who had forced himself upon me had been shot to death in a theater several months later by a man who was a complete stranger to him. And then after the basement incident, my father had been killed. I wondered at the connections.

Of course on the same day my father had been shot, a Lac-Mégantic police officer had also been killed. The funerals were the same day and the officers who had attended their comrade's funeral also attended my father's. They had all known him. As a show of respect for my father, they escorted his body to his final resting place. And as I imagined them in my mind, it seemed symbolic to me, the police taking my father away.

The contradictions of my father's life were inexplicable to me. I could remember him as a kind and decent man who loved his children and took pride in them. The world saw him as a friendly, generous, well-respected churchgoer and businessman. It was impossible to reconcile that Wellie Drouin with the monstrous one, the one who had almost killed me, the one behind the closed doors of our house, the one who drank and became transformed into a raging madman. I would never understand it. But on that day, standing in front of his grave, I forgave him. I forgave my father.

As I did so, I felt a weight lifting off me and I began to cry tears of relief and I felt a sense of peace and contentment come over me and I knew that my long journey had finally come to a close. Now, I could move on.

CHAPTER SEVENTEEN
Ellevie

∾

In Lac-Mégantic for two weeks with my brothers and sisters there were dinners and get-togethers and visits and drives around town. We talked sometimes about growing up in the Drouin house. None of us had a good childhood, I thought. "I don't ever remember being happy as a child," my oldest sister remarked. The details of the basement incident were sketchy for everyone, and that was fine with me. I knew enough.

I talked with my brother Robert about our father's death. He said he never blamed Philippe. Nobody did. In fact, Philippe would be released when he turned twenty-one. He's worked for the same company for more than forty-five years and has been married to the same woman for forty. They have two beautiful daughters and two grandchildren. But other than that short conversation with Robert, nobody in the family talks about the incident. Ever.

My sisters and I spent a day driving around Lac-Mégantic. We stopped in front of our house, the house with the basement. We didn't stop for long. I got out and took a picture. Two men were sitting on the small patio in front of the house. The house looked different, painted in blue. My memory was that it was a dark color. Standing out front, looking at the house, taking the picture, I didn't feel much of anything. The tension in the car was palpable.

Back in California, my life went on. I felt renewed. I felt strong. From time to time I thought about the long road to mental health that I had been on. I thought about the psychologists and psychiatrists and how instead of helping, they had collectively impeded my progress. But looking back, it seemed to me as if there was some kind of force guiding me forward, helping me to ever-so-slowly come to grips with my past. Things seemed to present themselves to me at times when I was most ready, and in the safest of places, like the memory of my grave coming to me in Dr. Andrew's waiting room. I thought of the dogs and how my eyes, by sheer chance one morning, had caught an advertisement for Afghan hounds, the one dog I was somehow not afraid of. I thought of losing my job for no apparent reason at J.C. Penney, only to end up working in a feed store where I was introduced to the feral cats who would start me on my kitten therapy. In hindsight it became clear to me that losing my job at J.C. Penney saved my life. Someone who saw the future was looking after me. Of that, I am certain. Too, I thought how I'd strangely felt compelled to travel all the way back to Lac-Mégantic where I was able to make peace with my parents, and by extension, my past—the final piece of the puzzle. All of this seemed to happen for me almost despite myself.

And I thought a lot about the little girl. Being buried alive, by all rights she probably should have died that night. Monsignor Bonin, delivering the last sacrament, must have thought so. It was a miracle that the little girl survived. But then, in a sense, she did die that night, alone and abandoned, only to be reborn thirty-five years later when it hit me that the girl in my vision was me. "She did not die," I cried that day in my kitchen.

And I wondered if, long ago, when she left the body and watched from above, did she in some way, somehow, remain above, watching over me? The guidance that I felt in my life, the force directing me—was it the little girl, somehow connecting me in a spiritual way to what the universe wanted for me? Was she connecting me to God? I'd often been angry at God, feeling as if He had sent me much more than I could handle. But in retrospect, was He there the whole time, along with the little girl from above?

Not long ago, I ordered a personalized license plate. I decided to combine my nickname Elle with Evie, my new middle name and name of the little girl: "Ellevie." One day, in a store parking lot, walking back to my car, I stopped dead in my tracks as I glimpsed the plate. I don't know why it hadn't struck me before. But somehow at that moment, I saw the name as if for the first time. "Ellevie." *Elle vie.* It's French. It means *she lives.*

– *The End* –

Time to Say Goodbye

∼

DISSOCIATIVE IDENTITY DISORDER (DID), WHAT I HAVE often referred to herein by its more common yet I suppose outdated name—Multiple Personality Disorder (MPD)—is clearly a controversial subject, within and without clinical psychology. Its diagnosis, treatment, and even its existence, remain hotly debated. I know from personal experience how complicated the disorder can be. I also know how frightening and confusing it can be. It's forgivable, and understandable, for the psychological profession to be somewhat at a loss over something so complex. What's less forgivable is the profession's arrogance in the face of such complexity. There is remarkably little humility for a group of professionals that, when it comes right down to it, know next to nothing about such a paralyzing mental disorder. Mental disorders are ostensibly the group's area of expertise.

I can't pretend that I can give advice to anybody who

might be suffering from something similar to what I struggled with for so much of my adult life. This book is a memoir, not a prescriptive book or a book meant to serve as a formula for treatment. I can only say that the company of my Afghan hounds and my work with the feral cats saved my life. My self-treatment did for me what clinical psychology could not. But I could never recommend it to others. Everyone is different. Everyone will react to different treatments in different ways. Humans are funny this way, a lesson the psychologists might consider, rather than pigeon-holing everyone with neat little labels, or simply relying on medication for the more frustrating cases, the ones that might actually take some effort and patience and expertise. I proved the doctor at Ross Valley wrong. I needed the drugs to function in life, he had written in my file. But I know I would not have survived the drugs.

My recovery was a long road. But in time, I was able to tear down, ever so gradually, the fortress that had protected the child abandoned so many years ago. And I was able to do so without having to entertain a therapist with the humiliating game-playing so often described in books by psychiatrists and psychologists. The task was often over-whelming, often dispiriting. But I never gave up and somehow I always knew that I would make it. What puzzles me most is that, if I was able to confront my nightmare past and learn to care for myself while at the same time being fully employed, earning management awards, serving on the boards of community organizations, and actively partici-pating in local politics, involving myself with human and animal rights issues—if I could do all that, why couldn't the professionals who study the human mind fulltime understand my struggle and see there are other ways to deal with such challenges besides drugging one into unconsciousness? When I think back to my forced stay at Ross Valley, I shudder.

My fervent hope is that the profession will one day find a suitable way to treat not just those suffering from DID, but from post-traumatic stress in general (the genesis, of course, of my particular experience with DID). The stakes are high. For my part, I was confused and frustrated. I didn't know how to get angry, or properly grieve. I think of those who tend towards anger and I can imagine their reactions to their post-traumatic stress veering into violence. I think of the recent mass shootings and I wonder what led the shooters to such deadly breaking points. Some of them were on medication. Surely we can do better.

Probably, it will only be a matter of time before adequate treatments are found. Yes, I have been critical of the profession, but I also know there are good, honest, committed people who are a part of it—people who are even now searching for ways to help those within their charge, to find better treatment methods, to find cures. These people will lead the way. They must.

As for me, I wish I could have found someone who could have helped me heal—faster and, perhaps, more completely. I have never been able to connect entirely with my seven-year-old self. To this day, she seems apart from me and I believe will remain so until the very day I die. My childhood, that is to say, remains lost. But if complete integration means having to relive the events of the basement and accept them, then I suspect that complete integration would be a backwards step. The memory was repressed for a reason. The repression was an effective—amazing—survival tool of a young mind under unthinkable duress. It was, contrary to its classification by the psychological profession, anything but a *disorder*. In any event, I have worked through the memory sufficiently to where I have gained back my peace of mind. I am no longer haunted by it.

As for my work with feral cats, it continued in earnest until 1997, working with Forgotten Felines and finding homes for hundreds of kittens over the years. I discovered the power of the Internet in 1994 when I launched a website dedicated to Sheba. By then I had bought a computer and taken a course in HTML. I told Sheba's story, as well as Little Evita's, and was stunned at how much they resonated with others. People all over the world cried for my dogs. (Of course I still had no apology from the veterinary community, nor from anyone else who had refused to help.) So in 1995, I posted the story of the little tabby online and received a similar response. Over the years, I've received literally thousands of emails from all over the world about Sheba and veterinary malpractice and of the account of the tabby and about feral cats in general. Although I no longer trap the cats or find homes for the feral kittens, I remain involved with feral cats and local politics. My city, the city of Petaluma, has banned feral cats from most areas, and traps and kills cats by the hundreds each year. They have made it illegal to feed outdoor cats. They have decided that birds in Shollenberger Park, a town boondoggle, have a greater right to life than cats, playing God with the animal population of the area. I give the cats a voice when I can. (More about my feral cat project can be found at www.petalumaferalcats.com.)

The Humane Society of Sonoma County was the only Society in California to be against two animal protection ballot measures decided (and passed) by voters in 1998. In a letter to me, Wayne Pacelle, then Senior Vice President of the Humane Society of the United States, wrote: "We were extremely disappointed that the Humane Society of Sonoma County took public stances against the two animal protection measures...We have communicated our strong disappointment to the Humane Society of Sonoma County."

In retrospect, my work with feral cats and my experiences with veterinary malpractice, make me wonder again at the chain of events of my life. My dogs and my work with the cats were of great comfort to me (and to the girls, of course) and the activism that came as a result was of enormous benefit to me. Why, it seems reasonable to ask, was I led here? To Petaluma, to Sonoma County? Was it the little girl? Was it God? Who can say? I can only marvel at a set of circumstances that somehow placed me where I felt most needed.

As for my ex-husband, James died in 2011 of complications from diabetes. He remained bitter about our divorce until his dying day. I felt sorry for him. He died alone. I hold no animosity towards him. I know full well that I was not an easy person to live with. James took on much more than he bargained for by marrying someone so complex and troubled. I know, too, that without him, without his financial support at the least, I could not have made it. I could not have raised four sons on my own and worked and been able to come to grips with my difficulties. I would have been institutionalized, maybe for good. I know the way James felt about the dogs and the cats and I know he had a good heart. Confused and often nonsensical, I was, perhaps, far above and beyond the call of standard husbandly duty. But with some emotional support from him, maybe the marriage would have been salvageable and not loveless.

My sons, too, tried to understand, but if I could not understand myself, I could not expect them to understand me, either. I did all I could to be the best mother to them that I could be, but the circumstances of my illness often made it difficult, if not impossible, to be everything that I would have loved to have been. If I have at all failed them, I hope they might now understand why.

I went to James's funeral in 2011. It was held in a church in Santa Rosa. I had never attended the church but when I walked in, the church, with its rich, beautiful wood, was immediately familiar to me. And I suddenly remembered a vision I had had back in 1975—one of the visions that had come to me during the est training: a vision of the very church I was standing in. I cannot explain it. Perhaps we have ways of being able to sometimes glimpse the future. I had died, after all, back in that basement. For how long, I do not know. Had I seen things? Glances of events to come? What was it that I said at Brookwood? I wonder still. I had spoken, perhaps, of a future tragedy. "How do you do that?" Dr. Chamberlin had asked me. Whatever was said, and however we acquire our knowledge of the world, I've learned this, if I've learned nothing else: the mind is an amazing, mysterious, and powerful thing.

As for the little girl, I don't think very often of her these days. She's at peace now, resting quietly, having been, first, remembered, and then cared for and comforted.

This past year, on my birthday, I felt compelled, for whatever reason, to listen to a favorite song of mine—Sarah Brightman and Andrea Bocelli's "Time to Say Goodbye". And as I did so, I quite unexpectedly felt the sudden presence of the twelve-year-old—the protector. Though the feeling was surprising, it was not disturbing or upsetting. And as the song continued to play, I felt the protector departing, leaving me for what I immediately understood would be forever.

I cried with mixed emotions. She had been in place to keep the past in the past, and she had performed her role in my life dutifully and capably, letting her guard down ever so slowly, bringing me only gradually in touch with the little girl, allowing it only when I was ready. She had no further part to play now. Her work had been done and by the end of the song, I knew she was gone.

The protector's gone. The little girl rests. It's just me now. And I'm at peace.

A final postscript: As the finishing touches were being put on the draft of this book, a tragedy was playing out in my childhood home of Lac-Mégantic. A train carrying seventy-two cars of crude oil was parked in the town of Nantes, seven miles away. Somehow, the brakes became disengaged. The train began rolling, picking up speed and derailing some eighteen minutes later in downtown Lac-Mégantic where it exploded into a vicious inferno. At least forty people were killed or missing, presumed dead. Because of the force of the explosion and the intensity of the heat from the ensuing flames, many bodies will probably never be found.

As it happens, the train derailed essentially in front of the house I lived in when I was seven—the house with the basement. The train continued its fiery slide as flames rose hundreds of feet into the night sky. Whole blocks of the city, containing many historical homes and buildings, were leveled. At the far end of the devastation was the home we lived in prior to the one when I was seven. The house I was born in. It sat across from the park where our parents would take us for walks. Both houses, and the park, were destroyed, swept away in a matter of moments by the raging fire.

1936
"The Way We Were"

This photo was taken at
Park des Vétérans, Lac Mégantic, Québec

(I am the baby standing beside my father)

July, 2013
The Bench

This photo was taken at the same location
Park des Vétérans, Lac Mégantic, Québec

A F T E R W O R D

My Work with Feral Cats

~

FOR CLOSE TO TWENTY YEARS, I WORKED ON MY "FERAL Cat Project," and at times utilizing the wonderful help of Forgotten Felines of Sonoma County, a non-profit organization dedicated to protecting and improving the lives of feral cats through local spay/neuter programs, placement services, community outreach, and nationwide education.

Recently I came across an article written by Jennifer Kirchner, Director for Forgotten Felines of Sonoma County. It reminded me of the ordeal I went through at the feed store, and a battle I had had years later with a very small local group against the City of Petaluma, which had banned all outdoor cats from most areas of the city. You can read about it at www.petalumaferalcats.com.

I strongly agree with Jennifer Kirchner's words (reprinted below with permission) and Forgotten Felines of Sonoma County about the feral cat and bird issue. It makes no sense at all to let cats breed and then kill them by the millions each year. Forgotten Felines of Sonoma County has the right idea and I encourage all to support and volunteer at your local organizations for a humane solution to control homeless pets in America.

February 11, 2013

Recently an article came out in the *New York Times* (and was reprinted locally) wherein the Smithsonian Conservative Biology Institute and the Fish and Wildlife Service state that cats, both free-roaming and pets, are responsible for killing 2.4 billion birds and 23.3 billion mammals each year.

Forgotten Felines of Sonoma County can't speak to where they are getting their "estimated" figures, or the validity of their data. Our position on this matter, which coincides with our mission, is as follows:

We do not believe in killing one creature to save another. The most <u>humane</u> way of controlling "community cats" (feral or free-roaming) is through trap, neuter, return—the method that we have been using since 1990 when we were founded. We are in complete agreement that:

Free roaming cats kill birds and small mammals—it is in their nature.

Indoor-only cats would be healthier, safer and would not impact our environment.

This is exactly why we work tirelessly to reduce the

free-roaming cat population. We care about ALL living beings—not <u>just</u> cats. This includes the impact that rounding up and killing cats has on us as human beings. Killing (not euthanizing) a viable, healthy, creature is bad. It's bad for the cat that is terrified up to the point that it is killed and it's bad for the shelter staff who have to house, then kill the cat. These people are members of our community and it's unconscionable to require them to take this action upon innocent creatures, day after day.

If the goal is to figure out what is happening to our world—whether it is a reduction in the bird population or destruction of our planet—we need only to look as far as the mirror.

Our goal is to reduce the feral cat population down to zero, but we can't do it alone.

Jennifer Kirchner

Executive Director

~

Please visit Jennifer's organization at www.forgotten-felines.com, and learn what you can do to help the feral cat population in your community. "Help us help them."

Marcelle Guy

ACKNOWLEDGMENTS

I WANT TO THANK MY FAMILY, MY BROTHERS AND SISTERS, for your understanding. This story was not easy to write and I know it cannot be easy for you to read, but I hope you will understand why I had to write it. My apologies if I cause anyone any pain.

Without the expert help and great patience from professional writer Jerry Payne, this book would not have been completed. Thank you, Jerry.

I met many people during my life but Eric Adams stands out as one of the kindest. A former journalist, accomplished writer, and movie director, it was his words of encouragement that drove me to write my story. Eric a million thanks to you.

I gratefully acknowledge everyone who walked with me through my life of recovery. You did not know it but you were helpful. There were times when I could not smile or look happy but you did not turn your back on me. You walked with me. I cannot name everyone for fear of forgetting someone but you know who you are: Employers, co-workers, neighbors, long-time and short-time friends. If we worked together you have in some way participated in my treatment and I want to thank you. Special thanks to Ione Gareis, Jean Burnett, Joan Herman, Mary Ryan and Connie Nicholson. We were the best crew and proved it year after year.

After retiring in 2009, the company of my friends helped me through some rough times. Writing this book was very emotional and thank heaven for friends: Bridget Mackay, I was not surprised to hear that you were voted best attorney. You have been so gracious and supportive. Kae Basque, Jo Ann Robertson, the walking/breakfast group, Lee Ann, Ida, Barbara, Jean and Joan, what terrific and understanding friends you have been. Lee Hamann, I am sure you thought I would never finish the book, let alone publish it, but here we are. I always look forward to our monthly chat over lunch.

Helder Rodriguez, Diane Reilly Torres, Mike Delaney, John Bertucci, I have learned so much from you as you freely shared your talents, your time and education with me.

I have met two exceptional human beings in the veterinary profession that I need to acknowledge here. Without them, I think I would have lost all faith in the human race. Dr. Douglas Blaine, DVM of Elk, California and Dr. Stanley Marks, DVM of the Veterinary Medical Teaching Hospital

University of California, Davis. When Sheba was misdiagnosed after the puppies were born, Dr. Blaine was so incensed at what was done to Sheba that he encouraged me to file a lawsuit against Dr. Skinner of the Redwood Veterinary Clinic in Santa Rosa, CA. He wrote a straightforward letter to the judge on my behalf. I think he knew he would be chastised by his colleagues but he did what was right.

Dr. Marks picked up Little Evita's treatment after being misdiagnosed by Dr. Michael Magne of the Sonoma County Emergency Clinic in Rohnert Park, CA. He faxed to me the results of Little Evita's necropsy. I think it was against the rules but, like Dr. Blaine, he was shocked at the wrong that was done and he spoke up. He did not speak of his feelings, but he shook my hand and held my hand for a while and I saw it in his eyes. After I read the necropsy I understood.

To Drs. Blaine and Marks, you have made such an impression on my spirit. I felt as if everyone was likely to lie and back a colleague no matter what. You showed me that there were good and honest veterinarians. I will remember your acts of integrity till the day I die. If I could, I would nominate you both for the RFK Award (if there was such award). We need more honest people like you to end the increasing corruption in today's world.

The last person to impact my life before this book goes to the printer, Nancy Cleary of Wyatt-MacKenzie, thank you for being there, Nancy. You and Jerry have been outstanding.

My most sincere thanks to you all. And a very special thanks to you, Alain.

"Every time we turn our heads the other way when we see the law flouted, when we tolerate what we know to be wrong, when we close our eyes and ears to the corrupt because we are too busy or too frightened, when we fail to speak up and speak out, we strike a blow against freedom and decency and justice."

~ ROBERT F. KENNEDY ~

CPSIA information can be obtained at www.ICGtesting.com
Printed in the USA
BVOW01*1634090614

355702BV00001B/1/P